Contents

On This Day

Irish Histories from *Drivetime*
on RTÉ Radio 1

Myles Dungan

Illustrations by Annie West

NEW ISLAND

ON THIS DAY
First published in 2015 by
New Island Books
16 Priory Office Park
Stillorgan
Co. Dublin
Republic of Ireland

www.newisland.ie

Print ISBN: 978-1-84840-484-7
Epub ISBN: 978-1-84840-485-4
Mobi ISBN: 978-1-84840-486-1

British Library Cataloguing Data.
A CIP catalogue record for this book is available from the British Library.

Typeset by JVR Creative India
Cover Design by Mariel Deegan
Printed by ScandBook AB, Sweden

Image of Dublin Castle courtesy of Thinkstock
Headshot of Michael Collins used with permission from National Library of Ireland
MGM Grand Lion Habitat by O. Palsson
Portrait of Lola Montez, 1847, by Joseph Karl Stieler

10 9 8 7 6 5 4 3 2 1

To Gwyneth Owen Máire Dungan Williams and her grandmother Máire – in honour of their only meeting on 26 April 2012.

Acknowledgements

My thanks are due to the Head of RTÉ Radio 1 Tom McGuire for permission to approach the producer of *Drivetime*, my good friend Tom Donnelly, with the proposal to revive the long-expired 'On This Day'. I am grateful to Tom Donnelly for running with the idea. But had he chosen not to do so he would still be a good friend.

To my RTÉ *History Show* producer Yetti Redmond for her encouragement and support. The fact that Yetti does 99.7 per cent of the work associated with the weekly radio exploration of our historical past allows me to indulge my 'On This Day' peregrinations and fancies.

I only write and read the scripts for 'On This Day'. The man who adds most of the value is my friend and frequent collaborator John Davis. My thanks to him for all the 'beds', 'SFX', 'twiddly bits' (sorry – that's a bewildering technical term) and inspired musical choices, which render these meanderings into actual broadcast material.

Thanks to Edwin Higel and Dan Bolger of New Island Books for taking this project on board. Some of the work I have enjoyed most has been with Edwin's trailblazing imprint.

To my adult children and full-time critics Amber, Rory, Lara and Ross, thanks for tuning in from time to time and surprising me by listening to these effusions with interest and amusement.

To my beloved wife and resident poet Nerys and our lovely bilingual (soon to be trilingual – she already has *amach, isteach, suas* and *síos*) daughter Gwyneth Owen, *diolch yn fawr iawn* for your support, love and entertainment.

Foreword

If you are going to steal an idea, make sure it's a good one. This entire book, and the radio segments on which it is based, is an excellent example of grand theft. In my youth I spent much time listening to morning radio programmes like the great Mike Murphy's *Morning Call,* produced by the late and equally great Gene Martin. I enjoyed on a daily basis the short items presented by, among others, P. P. O'Reilly. These short items recalled past events and brought them back to life on their anniversaries. They were entitled 'On This Day'.

'On This Day' was just too good an idea to leave in dignified retirement. It was just begging to be plagiarized. Somebody had to do it, didn't they? In the immortal words of Tom Lehrer, from the song 'Lobachevsky':

> *Plagiarize,*
> *Let no one else's work evade your eyes,*
> *Remember why the good Lord made your eyes,*
> *So don't shade your eyes,*
> *But plagiarize, plagiarize, plagiarize…*
> *Only be sure always to call it please, 'research'.*

Having now spent two years with this pirated idea, my main source of wonder is how the original writers managed to do it five days a week, fifty-two weeks a year. Producing one item a week for *Drivetime* is sufficiently enervating for this *soi-disant* historian. Not unlike a certain deity, though in inverse proportion, I find it best to labour for one day and rest for the other six.

This book is the product of two years (102 columns – with time off for good behaviour on Stephen's Day 2014 and Christmas Day 2015) of the revived 'On This Day' for the *Drivetime* programme. During that period most of the items have been introduced with great panache and energy by Mary Wilson, the programme's presenter, and more laconically, and with a certain detached scepticism, by Philip Boucher-Hayes, her accomplished deputy. (I do hope I have spelt his name correctly.) As Philip is my nephew he feels, naturally, entitled to maintain a certain familial distance from his uncle's dubious activities. I can only applaud his approach, while complaining to his mother.

It would be nice to claim these short essays as a microcosm of Irish history, but they are not. Their author has been circumscribed by the need to highlight only the events that have taken place on a Friday, the day of the week on which the item is invariably broadcast. While that is something of a nuisance – some days the material is more promising than others – the disadvantages are mitigated by the lack of any necessity to come up with a clever closing punch line. As with the originals of the species, each short column ends with those immortal words: '… XX years ago, on this day'. While it lacks the punch of 'the dog it was that died', it does prevent much unnecessary head scratching.

In addition, the material tends to reflect the prejudices, proclivities, partialities and areas of expertise of myself, the writer. Faced with three or four possible items, based on the activities of history makers on any particular day, I admit to doing something much beloved of the academic community, *viz.* 'favouring my research'. Readers, for example, may begin to notice the frequency with which variations on a theme of Charles Stewart Parnell appear in this slim volume.

No apology, however, (the previous paragraph was an apology in case you didn't notice) is made for the inclusion of a critical mass of material related to the Irish diaspora. While the stories of Irish achievements and disasters in the USA, Britain, Australia, Canada, India and elsewhere may not make it on to school and university history curricula in Ireland (insofar as a history curriculum continues to exist at second level), they will continue to figure in weekly 'On This Day' columns. I would venture to suggest that Irish people accomplished far more outside of their native land than they ever did within the confines of its hierarchical and traditionalist society. So tales of diasporic invention and re-invention abound and will continue as long as 'On This Day' survives.

The items included below are, more or less, as broadcast. A small number of errors have been uncovered and corrected. Doubtless others lie undetected. Small tweaks have been made to texts originally designed to be read aloud.

As a sometime historian and researcher it is truly delightful on this occasion to have been freed from the tyranny of the footnote. Graham Greene used to divide his *oeuvre* into two categories: 'novels' and 'entertainments'. This work definitely falls into the latter category. So if the reader is curious as to the source of certain items of information, he or she will, on this occasion, just have to take my word for it. The contents of every column may not prove to be entirely accurate, but I certainly have made nothing up. I will admit, though, that certain items of information, of slightly doubtful provenance, were just too good to be left out. Anything excessively dubious comes accompanied by a health warning.

January

Her name was Lola

23 January 1806
The Death of
William Pitt the Younger

Most British prime ministers, from the time the position was actually recognised until Irish independence in 1922, have had some influence, good or bad, on this country. Some found it difficult to avoid dealing with the perennial Irish Question. Others found it too much of a headache to be bothered engaging with Ireland and hoped it would simply go away. Some, like William Gladstone, had Ireland at the centre of the policies of three administrations.

William Pitt the Younger can probably be placed somewhere in the middle of the spectrum, with the boredom and irritation of Disraeli at one end and the positive engagement of Gladstone at the other. But he is best remembered in this country for a pivotal piece of legislation he pushed through and for his failure to deliver on an accompanying promise.

Although Pitt became Prime Minister in 1783 at the tender age of twenty-four, that is emphatically *not* why he was known as William Pitt the Younger. His callow youth could possibly have earned him the title 'William Pitt the *Young*', but not the comparative 'Pitt the *Younger*'. He was so-called to distinguish him from his father, William Pitt the Elder, who had become Prime Minister in 1866 when a comparatively long-in-the-tooth fifty-seven-year-old. Once again, though, that is *not* why he is called the *Elder*.

Pitt – the twenty-something version that is – came to power during trying times for Britain. Towards the middle of his tenure the French Revolution offered regular lessons to the plain people of Britain as to what they might want to do with their aristocrats if they got fed up with them. Just prior to his accession the unruly colonists on the far side of the Atlantic had decided they wanted to be American rather than British. On top of that Pitt had to deal with King George III, who had a tendency to go mad.

When a perfectly sane king appointed him Prime Minster in December 1783 no one predicted that the twenty-four-year-old would still be in power seventeen years later. His government was known as the 'mince pie administration' because it was assumed it would be 'cooked' by Christmas.

Pitt's impact on Irish history was profound. After the French Revolution, various wars with revolutionary France, and the 1798 Rebellion in Ireland, Pitt decided that the Irish parliament had to go. Ireland would have to be ruled directly from London and an Act of Union passed, which would see Irish MPs and Peers taking seats in the London parliament. Thousands of pounds were made available to bribe Irish grandees to vote their assemblies out of existence. Some of the bribery took the form of compensation to the owners of 'pocket boroughs' – electoral areas over which they had control – that would disappear with the passing of the Act of Union. This compensation was to be made available to those who opposed the union as well as to its supporters. There is no record of even the most vociferous antagonists of the proposed union throwing the tainted money back in the face of the government after the legislation passed in 1800. This was Ireland, after all, and even the rich were always happy to become a lot richer.

Where Pitt miscalculated was in offering Catholic Emancipation as part of the package. While this kept influential Catholics quiet, it infuriated a lot of ascendancy Protestants. Even more crucially, Pitt forgot to check with the King that His Madness would sign 'relief' for his Catholic subjects into law. Georgius Rex refused to countenance signing any such thing and Pitt, in a fit of integrity, resigned from office. Bizarrely, he had to stick around for a while before handing over power because the King had one of his bouts of insanity and couldn't appoint a successor. Eventually he was allowed to take his P45 and go.

He returned as Prime Minister in May 1804 but died in office two years later at the tender age of forty-six, two years older than Tony Blair was when he first assumed the office of Prime Minister in 1997, four days shy of his forty-fourth birthday.

William Pitt the Younger died two hundred and nine years ago, on this day.

Broadcast 23 January 2015

30 January 1846
The Birth of Katharine O'Shea

To this day she is known as Kitty, though her friends, family and London society in the late nineteenth century knew her as Katharine, or Kate. Although the name is innocuous today, during the Victorian era it was meant to sting – in those times 'kitty' was a euphemism for 'prostitute'.

She is at the heart of one of the great 'what ifs' of Irish history, as in 'what if Katharine O'Shea and Charles Stewart Parnell had never met?'

But meet they did. She was the wife, probably estranged at the time, of one of the great Irish chancers of Victorian London, Captain William Henry O'Shea, once a dashing Hussar but more familiar today as a talentless political opportunist. Had O'Shea not been a *failed* banker, he might well have found other ways in which to discommode his native country. But it was his failure as a politician that was to have more serious ramifications than his inadequacies as a financier.

In 1880 O'Shea was a rookie Irish MP; Parnell was the new leader of the Irish Parliamentary Party. O'Shea had an attractive wife and he obliged her to make herself useful in the advancement of his political ambitions. She was instructed to invite Parnell to a number of political soirées she organised on her husband's behalf. He pronounced his name as 'O'Shee', by the way, presumably to distinguish him from his common-or-garden countrymen of the same name. Parnell, however, was not one for the banality of opening invitations, or indeed letters in general. So, to press her invitations, Katharine went to see him in person. That, according to her account, was when they fell in love. Parnell didn't leave any account. He was as good at writing letters as he was at opening them.

The relationship blossomed rapidly and soon they were, in effect, man and wife. She became his 'Queenie'; he became her 'King'. O'Shea rarely darkened the door of his wife's boudoir but, nevertheless, found out about their trysts rather quickly. He challenged Parnell to a duel but when, to his surprise, the Irish party leader accepted the challenge, the former Hussar backed down. He contented himself thereafter with squeezing every drop of political nectar he could from his wife's lover and partner.

He looked away as the couple had three children together. His incentive for not divorcing Katharine, in addition to political advancement, was a hefty share in a large sum of money his estranged wife stood to inherit from an aged aunt. When the elderly lady finally passed on, and he was neatly cut out of the inheritance, he stopped looking away. He sued for divorce, no doubt full of the festive spirit, on Christmas Eve 1889.

The resulting court proceedings destroyed Parnell's career. In the middle of a year of already huge controversy in 1891, he only made things worse for himself politically when he married Katharine after the divorce was finalised. Humiliated by a series of futile and debilitating by-election campaigns, an exhausted Parnell died in their house in Brighton in October, a month the highly superstitious Parnell had always considered ill-starred.

Katharine Parnell, as she now was, then did a great service to a country that she had never visited and much of whose population considered her to be either a scarlet woman or an English spy who had destroyed their great leader. In an act of generosity, she waived her right to have Parnell buried in a South of England graveyard where she could join him when her own life ended. Instead, she allowed him to be returned to Ireland and interred in Glasnevin cemetery, in perhaps the biggest funeral the country had ever seen.

Katharine O'Shea, or Katharine Parnell as she chose to be called, was born five months before her second husband, Charles Stewart Parnell, one hundred and sixty-nine years ago, on this day.

Broadcast on 30 January 2015

17 January 1861
The Death of Lola Montez

The story of Lola Montez is full of untruths and myths – she made up most of them herself. Even the time and place of her birth is disputed. She was born in Limerick in 1818 or Grange, Co. Sligo in 1821. It doesn't help that she consistently lied about her age.

Nominally a dancer (her dancing skills were, apparently, negligible), she was, in fact, one of the most sought-after courtesans of her era. Through a combination of good looks, charm and supreme self-confidence, she managed to inveigle her way into the upper reaches of European and American society in the nineteenth century. Along the way she reinvented herself more often than a nervous chameleon.

Among her celebrated European conquests were King Ludwig of Bavaria, Tsar Nicholas I of Russia and Alexandre Dumas, the author of the *Three Muskateers*. Her unique selling point as a performer was the Tarantula Dance (also known as the Spider Dance). This involved the sudden 'discovery' in the course of a terpsichorean routine of a large furry 'spider' in her clothes. It was actually a facsimile arachnid made of rubber, cork and whalebone. Her frenzied attempts to remove the 'spider', of course, necessitated the removal of much of her clothing. This made her very popular indeed with men right across the continent of Europe.

Sometime in the 1850s she decamped to the USA and eventually arrived in the burgeoning city of San Francisco. She sought to create a sensation and didn't have to try very hard. Whenever she ventured out she was accompanied by two greyhounds. A parrot adorned her shoulder. She made good copy.

She quickly snared the publisher and former gold rush miner Patrick Hull. The attraction, she claimed, was based on his ability to tell a funny story. He must have run out of jokes fairly rapidly as the relationship was quickly on the rocks. When other female artistes began to send up the Spider Dance in their own acts, Lola took to the road.

In 1854 she embarked on a tour of the music and concert halls of the mining towns of California. But the boom-towns were not as susceptible to Lola's charms as the slightly more sophisticated San Francisco. Some of the miners, unimpressed by her dancing skills, booed her off the stage. Lola didn't take all this lying down. A newspaperman who gave her a bad review was threatened with a horsewhipping while a second was challenged to a duel.

In the past, Lola had demonstrated that such threats of physical violence were not all merely aggressive bluster. She had once horse-whipped a theatre manager and had broken the nose of her agent with a heavy brass candlestick.

After an unsuccessful tour Lola settled down near the mining town of Grass Valley in Northern California. One story about her that gained local currency was that she habitually bathed in champagne and dried her much-admired body with rose petals. She is also said to have shared her life with a pet bear. But all this could not last; the money ran out and she was soon on the road again.

By the end of her life Lola was so far down on her luck that she passed away in a dilapidated boarding house in the notorious Hell's Kitchen area of New York City. She was forty years old ... or thirty-eight ... or forty-two.

Lola Montez died one hundred and fifty-three years ago, on this day.

Broadcast 17 January 2014

9 January 1873
The Birth of John J. Flanagan,
Irish-American Hammer-Thrower

They were known as the 'Irish Whales': John J. Flanagan, Matt McGrath, Jim Mitchell, Patrick J. Ryan and Con Walsh. In the early years of the twentieth century these Irishmen, all domiciled in the USA, ruled the world of hammer throwing, winning five Olympic gold medals between them. But it was Flanagan, born in Kilbreedy, near Kilmallock, Co. Limerick in 1873, who was *primus inter pares.*

Flanagan, who, for a successful field athlete, stood a relatively modest 5'10, was something of an all-rounder. He had already established his reputation in field sports before he emigrated to the USA in 1896. There he began to specialise in the hammer event which, in 1900, was included in the programme for the Paris Olympic Games. Flanagan, the world-record holder, represented the USA and beat two other American throwers to take the first hammer gold with a throw of just over fifty-one metres. He was the only American who was not attending university to win a medal at those games. Both the silver and bronze medallists in his event, Truxton Hare and Josiah McCracken, were college football players.

He repeated the feat in the St Louis games in 1904, once again taking gold from two Americans. His third and final gold medal, at the London Olympics in 1908, must have given him a great deal of satisfaction. A section of the crowd appeared to dislike the idea of an Irishman competing for the USA at the Olympic Games and made their feelings clear, vocally, by booing the Limerickman. Flanagan defied their disapproval to take the laurels with a throw of almost fifty-two metres. Fellow Irishman Matt McGrath took the silver, which must really have pleased the home crowd. Their cup surely ran over entirely when the bronze was hung around the neck of Con Walsh, competing for Canada.

Flanagan and McGrath (who himself won Olympic gold in 1912) were both members of the New York Police Department. Flanagan's first posting was something of a sinecure. He worked in the Bureau of Licences, where he had a lot of time on his hands. This was mostly used for training at the Irish American Athletic Club in Queens.

Flanagan was a committed competitor no matter what the occasion. In 1905, during a police sports meeting in New York, he dominated the throwing events as expected. That, however, wasn't enough for him, and to demonstrate that he also possessed a turn of speed he entered and won the inelegantly titled Fat Man's Race.

In 1910 he ended his career as one of New York's finest after he was transferred to West 68th street and forced to walk a beat near Central Park.

Flanagan, in addition to his three Olympic golds, won nine US championships and set thirteen world records. In 1911 he returned to Ireland and a few years later took over the family farm on the death of his father. He died, aged seventy-five, on 4 June 1938 in his native Limerick.

Inspired, no doubt, by his superhuman achievements, there is a belief that Flanagan's middle name was Jesus. This is how he appears on the Olympic.org website. But it seems his middle name was, in fact, the far humbler and more mundane, Joseph.

The first occasion on which the hammer event at the Olympic Games was NOT won by an athlete competing for the USA was in 1928, when Pat O'Callaghan, throwing for Ireland, took the gold. This would have been an immensely satisfying moment for Flanagan, as he was O'Callaghan's coach.

Irish-born Olympian, John J. Flanagan, was born one hundred and forty-two years ago, on this day.

Broadcast 9 January 2015

2 January 1880
Charles Stewart Parnell's Visit to the USA Begins

When asked by a customs official, on his arrival in New York in the 1880s, did he have anything to declare, a celebrated Irish Protestant and aristocratic gentleman claimed to have uttered the immortal phrase: 'I have nothing to declare but my genius'. But Charles Stewart Parnell was not Oscar Wilde and, unlike the yet-to-be famous writer, the Irish politician was not there to fundraise for himself, but for a political cause to which he had become aligned the previous year: the struggle for ownership of the land of Ireland.

Parnell, as yet an aspiring rather than actual political leader, was President of the Irish Land League. The Land War was proving to be an expensive and potentially ruinous campaign and the main potential source of funds was the Irish community in the USA. So, in December 1879, Parnell traversed the Atlantic to tap into the latent Anglophobia of Irish-America.

Parnell had many familial links and at least one romantic association with the USA. His mother Delia Tudor Stewart was the daughter of an American admiral who had fought the British in the War of 1812. Parnell's innate contempt of the English was probably genetic, inherited from his Anglophobic mother.

The romantic association originated in Paris where he had met a young American woman, a Miss Woods, from Rhode Island. There was talk of an engagement. There was certainly an understanding of some sort. When her family journeyed from France to Italy Parnell followed. In Rome, however, he was overcome by his infamous hypochondria. His fear of fever prompted him to return to Ireland.

Miss Woods and her family sailed for the USA. Parnell followed her to Rhode Island. There she informed him that she did not wish to marry him as 'he was only an Irish gentleman without any particular name in public'. She repented of her injudicious rejection at her leisure. By the time of Parnell's triumphant and very public tour of the USA in 1880 Miss Woods was married, but she admitted to Parnell's brother John, who visited her in Newport, that she regretted not accepting Parnell's proposal. How different Irish history might have been had she done so.

Like Oscar Wilde after him, Parnell set off on a nationwide fundraising tour. His topic, however, was not aesthetics, but rack-renting, evictions, boycotting and Home Rule. Such was the level of publicity attracted by this very American Irishman that he was permitted to address the members of the US House of Representatives. It was not his finest hour as a public speaker. Up to that point in his career he had had few particularly fine rhetorical moments; he had yet to conquer a native stiffness and crippling nervousness to become the celebrated orator of later life. But at least he was addressing one of the houses of the US Congress.

As the tour progressed and he travelled further from the East Coast, Parnell's rhetoric became more extreme. By the time he reached Cincinnati, Ohio, in the last week of February, he was talking about destroying 'the link which keeps Ireland bound to England'. The longer the Irish-American pilgrimage went on, however, the more shambolic it became. To save the day a young Timothy Healy was brought over from Ireland to get Parnell organised. He was not there for long but he was responsible for at least one enduring slogan. On 7 March in Montreal Healy coined the phrase 'the Uncrowned King of Ireland' in describing Parnell to his audience. Given their later spectacular falling-out, Healy probably regretted that particular piece of hyperbole. He did atone for it in 1891 by calling Parnell all manner of uncomplimentary things – including labelling him a thief.

The trip ended abruptly on 8 March when a telegram from Ireland informed Parnell that Disraeli had called an early general election. A few months later he would win the chairmanship of the Irish Parliamentary Party and begin the drive towards land reform and Home Rule.

Charles Stewart Parnell began his triumphant if somewhat disorganised tour of the USA one hundred and thirty-five years ago, on this day.

Broadcast 2 January 2015

3 January 1920
Recruitment Begins for the
Black and Tans

In January 1920 the British government placed advertisements in newspapers for men who were willing to 'face a rough and dangerous task'. The jobs on offer were as Temporary Constables in the Royal Irish Constabulary, a force by then coming under intense pressure from the IRA.

The target market for the advertisements was unemployed ex-servicemen, men who knew how to handle weapons and men who had survived the horrors of the Great War. Recruits, around 7,000 altogether, were trained for about three months and then sent to Ireland. Such a large influx caught the RIC unawares and a lack of uniforms meant the temporary constables were dressed in khaki trousers and dark police tunics. Their attire reminded a Limerick journalist, Christopher O'Sullivan, of the colouring of the Kerry Beagles that made up the famous Black and Tan hunt on the Limerick/Tipperary border. The name stuck. They were paid ten shillings a day plus board and lodging at a time when the pay for a British army private was little more than a shilling a day.

Never noted for their military discipline, despite their backgrounds, the RIC Temporary Constabulary took to the unofficial reprisal with gusto. It was Black and Tan units who torched Balbriggan and assisted in the burning of Cork city centre. The latter escapade razed to the ground more than 300 buildings in the southern capital. Those responsible proudly displayed burnt corks in their caps for a time thereafter.

A few myths have grown up about the Tans. For a start, they were not all British. At least ten per cent of the members of the force were Irish-born. Neither were they responsible for the shooting of civilians on Bloody Sunday in Croke Park; that was largely the work of the even more vicious RIC Auxiliary Division, the notorious 'Auxies'. Neither did Tom Barry 'lay all the Black and Tans low' at the Kilmichael ambush in 1920, as the words of the song would have it. The seventeen security force fatalities on that day were also Auxiliaries.

But during the War of Independence, better known at the time as 'the Tan war', no one really made too many distinctions between the various forces who terrorised the towns and villages of the country. Their philosophy, insofar as they can be described as philosophers, was encapsulated in the address of an RIC Commander to Listowel policemen in June 1920. He insisted that suspicious-looking persons should be shot on sight. 'You may make mistakes occasionally,' he continued, 'and innocent persons may be shot, but that cannot be helped, and you are bound to get the right parties some time.'

In a gesture of sweet irony, the 'Cogadh na Saoirse' medal, awarded since 1941 by the Irish government to IRA veterans of the War of Independence, includes a ribbon with two vertical bands; the stripes are in black and tan.

The name itself is still to be found in use in various forms in the USA. In 2006 Ben and Jerry's got themselves in hot water when they created a new ice cream called 'Black and Tan'. It doesn't appear to have caught on. Two years ago Nike thought better of referring to a new brand of trainers as a 'Black and Tan' after protests from Irish-American groups.

Recruitment advertisements for the infamous RIC temporary constabulary were up and running in British newspapers ninety-four years ago, on this day.

Broadcast 3 January 2014

24 January 1920
The Death of Performer and Composer Percy French

When the singer-songwriter Don McClean, creator of 'American Pie' – the song, not the film – had an international hit with 'The Mountains of Mourne', most of his worldwide fans assumed that he had written it himself. Few, outside of Ireland, had ever heard of Percy French: humourist, civil engineer, songwriter, landscape painter, banjo player, poet, inspector of public drains and sometime musical hall performer.

French was born in Cloonyquinn House, Roscommon, in 1854, into a landowning family. He wrote his first song, 'Abdul Albulbul Amir', before he even went to university, and had an early experience of what it was like to be ripped off when he sold it for £5 and later saw others claim it as their own composition.

After leaving Trinity College, Dublin in the mid 1870s he took a job inspecting drains with the Office of Public Works in Co. Cavan. During his time spent peering into other people's sewage he wrote many of his most famous tunes and painted prodigiously.

His employment with the OPW lasted until 1887. He was laid off when the organisation downsized. To keep body and soul together French decided to combine some of his emerging talents and established a comic magazine, *The Jarvey*. It was only when that unhappy enterprise failed that he really launched his career as a songwriter and entertainer. This was in spite of the huge tragedy of his life: the loss of his young wife, Ettie, in 1891. She died in childbirth at the age of twenty and their baby daughter died a few days later. French remarried in 1894 to Helen Sheldon and went on to have three daughters.

His better-known songs are generally comic or sentimental. 'The Mountains of Mourne', a song of emigration and nostalgia, was written in 1896. His hymn to the county that first employed him, 'Come Back Paddy Reilly to Ballyjamesduff', was penned in 1912. (An excellent statue of French can be found sitting on a park bench in the main street of Ballyjamesduff.) By the early 1900s he was a popular music hall performer, touring the world with his partner and accompanist Dr W. Houston Collison.

His most celebrated comic song was written as sweet revenge. 'Are You Right There, Michael?' famously parodies the notoriously tardy West Clare railway service. In 1897 French travelled on the line from an engagement in Sligo to one in Clare. The service was so slow, with the driver making numerous unexplained and unscheduled stops, that by the time French arrived at the venue for the 8.00 p.m. recital, the audience had gone home. West Clare railway attempted to sue him for libel due to the subsequent ridicule to which they were subjected, but they were, fortunately for French, unsuccessful.

An anecdote, probably apocryphal, but too good not to recount, tells of how French was late for his day in court. On being admonished by the judge he replied, 'I apologise, Your Honour, but I travelled here by the West Clare railway'.

Percy French died ninety-four years ago, on this day.

Broadcast 20 January 2014

16 January 1922
Michael Collins Takes Possession of Dublin Castle

Michael Collins accurately concluded in December 1921 that in agreeing to the terms of the Anglo-Irish Treaty he had signed his own death warrant. But without having appended his signature to the document on 6 December 1921, he would not have been able to participate in an event six weeks later that must have given him a great deal of satisfaction.

Once the Treaty was signed and ratified by Dáil Éireann on 7 January, the British didn't really hang around, bar a port or two, the loan of some artillery to start the Civil War, and of course the six counties. The new rulers of Ireland were instructed to be ready to take over Dublin Castle in mid-January.

There could be no clearer indication of the actual intention of the British to leave the twenty-six county Irish Free State than the handing over of this sprawling monument to British rule in Ireland. For centuries Ireland had been governed from 'The Castle'. Members of the majority religion who co-operated with the British administration to their financial benefit were known as 'Castle Catholics'. Everything British that had its being in Ireland emanated from 'The Castle'.

Built at the behest of King John in the 13th century to provide a base for the English conquest of the rest of the country from Dublin, it had remained the nexus of English and then British rule, as well as the abiding symbol of the colonisation of Ireland. The castle has been witness to several fascinating events that have given it such a colourful history. It was from the Bermingham Tower in Dublin Castle that the legendary escape of Red Hugh O'Donnell and Art O'Neill took place in the depths of winter, January 1592. Art O'Neill perished in the Dublin Mountains, but O'Donnell managed to make his way to the sanctuary of the O'Byrne's in Glenmalure, Co. Wicklow. Just over 200 years later, in 1907, the Insignia of the Order of St Patrick, known as the Irish Crown Jewels, were stolen from the Bedford Tower in an audacious robbery that has never been solved. Half of Dublin at the time knew who had stolen them. The problem was they nominated the other half of the city as the thieves.

The castle might well have fallen during the upheavals of 1641, but it did not succumb to rebel control. Robert Emmett could conceivably have taken it in 1803, but dismally failed to do so. It was even more vulnerable in 1916, but the Volunteers failed to walk the ball into an open goal.

So Michael Collins, dressed impressively in his military uniform, must have savoured the moment when his staff car drove into the precincts of the complex of buildings whose fabric he had successfully managed to infiltrate during the Anglo-Irish war. He himself had somehow managed to stay out of the clutches of its more sinister and homicidal operatives.

When Collins stepped out of his staff car he was greeted waspishly by the Lord Lieutenant, Lord Fitzalan. 'You are seven minutes late, Mr Collins', observed His Majesty's last Viceroy in Ireland. The Irish leader is said to have responded acidly, 'We've been waiting over seven hundred years, you can have the seven minutes.'

Fitzalan, the first Catholic Lord Lieutenant since the reign of King James II, then took Collins on an impromptu tour of the facility before absenting himself and leaving Collins, literally, holding the fort.

Michael Collins took possession of Dublin Castle on behalf of the Irish provisional government, ninety-three years ago, on this day.

Broadcast on 16 January 2015

10 January 1952
The Crash of the Aer Lingus Plane
the *St Kevin*

When we think of plane crashes and Aer Lingus, the one that immediately comes to mind is the mysterious 1968 Tuskar Rock disaster. In circumstances that are, as yet, largely unexplained, the Viscount aircraft, the *St Phelim* (flight EI-712), fell from the sky as it cruised towards the coast of Wales. For years, rumours abounded that the *St Phelim* had been shot down by a missile launched during a British military exercise. In recent years an investigation has suggested that the reason for the crash was more banal, involving simple structural failure.

But the Tuskar Rock crash was not a first for Aer Lingus.

The company began operations in May 1936 and it was almost sixteen years before its first fatal air disaster, in January 1952. It was one of sixty-five fatal crashes that year. To put that figure in some perspective, over the last three years, with air traffic having increased exponentially since the 1950s, there has been an average of thirty-five fatal incidents a year.

On 10 January 1952, at 5.25 p.m., the *St Kevin*, a DC-3 (flight EI-AFL) took off from Northolt airport near London. Northolt, now an RAF base, was being used by commercial aircraft during the construction of Heathrow. The weather was bad, and further deteriorated as the aircraft approached the Welsh coast. The rain was torrential and the winds were close to gale force.

Shortly after 7 p.m. the pilot, Captain James Keohane, reported to the Nevin Radio station, south of Anglesey, that he had reached the Irish Sea and requested permission to descend from 6,500 to 4,500 ft. It was the last ever transmission from the *St Kevin*. Its intended route should have taken it fifteen miles south of Mount Snowdon. In fact, far from being over the Irish sea, the plane was heading almost directly towards the 3,650ft high peak. A few minutes later it crashed into the bleak and bare Cwm Edno valley, a few miles from the highest point in Wales. All twenty passengers on board and the three crew members were killed.

First news of the disaster came with a telephone call to Carnarvon police from two locals who told of having seen and heard a plane crash. Rescuers reported a scene of devastation when they reached the crash site after first light the following morning, having climbed for almost an hour to get there. Sections of the wreckage and many of the bodies had been sucked into the marshy soil of the high valley. One poignant account reported how a child's doll had been thrown clear of the burning wreckage, a sight that was particularly distressing for the recovery party. The doll belonged to five-year-old Melody Laker. Her parents were also on board, having decided at the last minute to take their daughter with them to Ireland. Her father, Michael, was himself an Aer Lingus pilot.

Among the other victims was a sixteen-year-old German girl, Lily Wenman, on her way to Dublin to live with her grandmother, Evelyn Belton, cousin of a former Lord Mayor of Dublin. Another casualty was the twenty-three-year-old air hostess, Deirdre Sutton, who had only been working for Aer Lingus for two years.

Accident investigators concluded that 'the encountering of a powerful down-current of air on the lee-side of Snowdon forced the aircraft down into an area of very great turbulence where the pilots lost control'. At the time of the accident it was one of the tenth worst in British aviation history – even today it remains in the top thirty. Twelve of the victims of the crash, including Captain Keohane, Melody Laker and her mother Dorothy, are buried in a communal grave in the parish cemetery of Llanbeblig in Carnarvonshire. Michael Laker's body, like that of a number of other victims, was never recovered. A stone memorial was placed in the ground close to the crash site at Cwm Edno in the wild and beautiful Snowdonia National Park.

The *St Kevin* made its final fateful flight from London to Dublin, sixty-two years ago, on this day.

Broadcast 10 January 2014

February

Jim 'Lugs' Branigan and colleagues "Going to a Wedding"

20 February 1794
The Birth of Writer William Carleton

One of the great Irish writers of the nineteenth century, William Carleton, worked as a clerk in a Church of Ireland Sunday school office, but is most famous for the first book he ever published, *Traits and Stories of the Irish Peasantry,* which came out when he was in his early thirties. To literate Dubliners, Carleton was a Protestant writer who was noted for his satirical takes on certain Roman Catholic rituals, such as penitential pilgrimages to Lough Derg. By the 1830s Carleton was a well-regarded, middle-class, Protestant writer with an eye for detail and dialogue, who had managed to capture the vagaries, eccentricities and violent tendencies of the Irish Catholic peasant.

This is why Carleton's real background is doubly interesting. He was born into Catholic peasant stock in Co. Tyrone in 1794. He received much of his education in a variety of local hedge schools – informal educational establishments of an era prior to organised primary education. His early life was far from unproblematic. His family was evicted from their smallholding in 1813. Carleton himself, despite his later impeccable Protestant respectability, had at one time been a member of a local agrarian secret society.

When his academic abilities had been noted, it appeared that Carlton was set for the priesthood. But rather than follow the road laid down for him by birth, tradition, and the will of others, Carlton made his own decisions. If we are to believe the story of

31

'The Poor Scholar', he reacted against the idea of the priesthood after being discouraged by a portentous dream.

He left Tyrone in 1817 and worked as a hedge-school master himself for a time before trying his luck in Dublin. He had little more than half a crown in his pocket when he arrived in a city in decline post the 1800 Act of Union. His luck held, he made some opportunistic adjustments to his life and prospered for a while, despite some early failures. He sought to join the army, for example, but it was suggested to him by a regimental colonel that such a life might not be the best one for him. He had made his application in Latin.

Carleton has given us characters like Willie Reilly and his dear Colleen Bawn, as well as the Squanders of Castle Squander. He also wrote a fictionalised but searing account of the Great Famine, *The Black Prophet*, published in the dark year of 1847.

Never a man given to political consistency, he once wrote to Sir Robert Peel (who was Home Secretary at the time and would later become Prime Minister), offering to link Daniel O'Connell to agrarian and anti-Protestant crimes while still managing to befriend the romantic nationalists of Young Ireland and contribute to their newspaper, *The Nation*. Despite, or perhaps because of, his own Catholic birth, his writing on the subject of religion and politics was virulently anti-Roman.

He died in 1869, the year William Gladstone disestablished the Church which he had joined in the 1820s. Never good with money, he had relied in the twilight of his life on a government pension after a successful petition from a wide range of Irish political and religious figures, including the fiery Belfast Protestant evangelical preacher Dr Harold Cooke, and the President of the Roman Catholic seminary at Maynooth College.

Carleton never quite extracted his foot entirely from the camp into which he was born, in Clogher, Co. Tyrone, two hundred and nineteen years ago, on this day.

Broadcast 20 February 2015

Bir

Not man
own lifetii
Born into
and educat(
the most in   ....th century
and one of   g...ificant entrepreneurs and
philanthropis

the Dublin–Kingstown line. The strike
to pay his employees based on their
with the strike, Dargan's workers
the delicately nurtured inhab
bathing in the sea during
as 'an indelicate state'
Dargan was re
miles of railw
other hug
Lough
no

Showing early promise as a mathematician, he then trained as a surveyor thanks to the generosity of, among others, the MP Henry Parnell. Later he found work with the famous Scottish engineer Thomas Telford in the building of the London to Holyhead road in the early 1820s. Moving back to Ireland, he earned the large sum of £300 for his work on a new road from Raheny to Sutton, near Dublin, which served the Howth mail-packet station. The money was used as seed capital to fund many future projects. These included the building of Ireland's first railway line in 1831, from Dublin to what was then Kingstown and what is now Dun Laoghaire.

While Dargan did not acquire the same sort of reputation as an employer as did another well-known Irish railway builder, William Martin Murphy, he did manage to antagonise some of his workers into a week-long strike during the construction of

ended when he agreed
productivity. Unconnected
managed to scandalise some of
tants of South County Dublin by
their lunch breaks in what was described

sponsible for the construction of almost 1,000
y line in Ireland and for the building of, amongst
projects, the Ulster Canal between Lough Erne and
Neagh. He also reclaimed land in Belfast Lough, on which
stands the Harland and Wolff shipyard.

Dargan, although well insulated by his growing wealth, lived through the horrors of the Great Famine. He was instrumental in restoring some of the country's morale in the wake of that catastrophe when he spent £100,000 on the Dublin Industrial Exhibition of 1853, located on what is now Leinster Lawn, overlooking Merrion Square. At its conclusion, a new National Gallery was built on the site. Today the gallery contains a Dargan wing and the statue of the great engineer, which was erected near the front entrance and unveiled in 1863. The iconic Luas bridge in Dundrum, completed in 2004, is also named after him. The Nine Arches viaduct in Milltown, still used today in running the Luas line, is yet another of Dargan's constructions.

As would William Martin Murphy in 1907, Dargan declined a knighthood more than half a century before. In 1853, on one of her four visits to the country, Queen Victoria actually came to call on Dargan in his mansion at Mount Anville. She sought to make him a baronet. Again he declined the offer.

Dargan was renowned for his humanity and generosity in his dealings with businesses on the brink of extinction during and after the Famine. This may not have been entirely altruistic. He is reputed to have observed on occasions that 'a spoonful of honey will catch more flies than a gallon of vinegar'. When he died in 1867 he had acquired a reputation as 'The Workman's Friend', having provided employment to thousands. His funeral was, reportedly, the largest in Dublin since that of Daniel O'Connell twenty years before.

William Dargan, railway builder, businessman and philanthropist, was born two hundred and fifteen years ago, on this day.

Broadcast 28 February 2014

13 February 1820
The Death of Barrister, Composer and Informer Leonard McNally

There are spies, there are informers, there are traitors, and then there is Leonard McNally. He was one of the most effective and enduring British spies in the ranks of an Irish revolutionary organisation. The unlucky, or careless, rebels were the United Irishmen, the men of 1798.

McNally, a barrister and playwright, was actually a prominent and radical member of the United Irishmen himself. He was eager for the organisation to accept military assistance from revolutionary France. But when William Jackson, an agent of the French government, was arrested in Ireland in 1794, McNally, rather than wait to be shopped for treason by Jackson, took a more pro-active course and offered his services to the Crown in exchange for not being hanged, drawn and quartered. Given what actually happens to someone who is hanged, drawn and quartered, he might well be forgiven for this initial capitulation. But the fact that he was still providing intelligence to Dublin Castle a quarter of a century later suggests that his collaboration had become more about remuneration than self-preservation.

After the 1798 Rebellion McNally defended many United Irishmen charged with involvement in the abortive insurrection. He didn't win a single case. It could have been because his clients were guilty to begin with, or because he was fiendishly unlucky. But his winless streak was more likely to have been related to the fact that he was passing information on his clients to the prosecution. Not really the done thing for a defence attorney, as I'm sure you'll agree.

Among the men he defended were William Jackson, Wolfe Tone, Lord Edward Fitzgerald and, in 1803, Robert Emmet. So, were there an Irish Pantheon, he would probably have contributed to the presence of about half the occupants. In the case of Emmet he advised the Crown that his client would enter no defence and allow cross-examination of no witnesses on his behalf, as long as prosecution witnesses did not misrepresent the facts. So the trial would be a walkover for the prosecution; Dublin Castle didn't even have to bother fabricating evidence that might come back to haunt them in court.

After 1803 you'd have thought McNally would have quietly and gracefully retired. But a £200 bonus, on top of his hefty pension of £300, ensured that 'J.W.' – the code name by which he was known to his spymasters – stayed in business until his death in 1820.

In a doubtlessly fruitless effort to mitigate McNally's evil reputation, it should be pointed out that he was also a successful playwright and librettist. One of his songs, 'The Lass of Richmond Hill', became a huge hit in its day, 1789, and a favourite of King George III. It was written about McNally's first wife, Frances, and describes her as 'a rose without a thorn'.

In one of those wonderful ironies for which a fiction writer would be pilloried were it to appear in a novel, a legal treatise, written by McNally the year before his betrayal of Robert Emmet, was pivotal in the definition of the principle of guilt being 'beyond reasonable doubt' before conviction.

His espionage activities did not become apparent until after his death when his son sought to have the payment of his pension continued *post mortem*. When the Lord Lieutenant, Earl Talbot, inquired as to why a pension had been paid to such an ardent nationalist, the truth began to emerge.

Leonard McNally, barrister, playwright, serial informer and a rose with many thorns, died one hundred and ninety-five years ago, on this day.

Broadcast 13 February 2015

14 February 1856
The Birth of Writer and Controversialist Frank Harris

Around the time of the foundation of the Irish State, it would probably have come as a surprise to many Irish people that the notorious Frank Harris, the author of 'that filthy book' *My Life and Loves*, was also a compatriot. But indeed he was. The only mitigating factor in his otherwise unrelievedly Irish origins was that his parents were Welsh, his father being a naval officer from Fishguard. This probably had little to do with his voracious sexual appetite and his repeated committal of his sexual history to paper. He had a reputation in the 1890s of being 'the best talker in London', at a time when Oscar Wilde, George Bernard Shaw and Winston Churchill provided stiff competition for the title.

Harris, fêted by some as a writer who pushed out the boundaries of journalism, and loathed by many more as a rampant pornographer, was born in 1856 in Galway. It was his departure from Ireland at the tender age of twelve that began the process that would result in the publication of *My Life and Loves*. He was sent to school in Wales, didn't like it, and ran away after a year. Most callow teenagers would have headed for Cardiff, or London if they were more adventurous. Harris, however, travelled to America. There he held down a number of menial jobs before finding his feet in the American Wild West in the 1870s; by working as a cowboy.

He was inveigled into that hazardous profession by a man known only as Mexican Bob. The dangers of the open range included weather, wildlife (literally and metaphorically), water, women, weapons and wrongdoing. Despite his subsequent notoriety, Harris managed to avoid the metaphorical wildlife; his youth meant he steered clear of cow-town women and a range of colourful and painful venereal diseases. But he almost succumbed to the literal variety when bitten by a rattlesnake. Only the attentions of two colleagues kept him alive. As in much of his literary output, Harris was prone to exaggerate his western adventures. He describes, for example, one incident in which he claimed that he and four other cowboys managed to hold off a one-hundred-strong raiding party of Native Americans.

On returning to the UK, Harris became a successful journalist, his greatest achievement probably being his editorship of the *Saturday Review*, a periodical that included H.G.Wells and George Bernard Shaw as contributors.

Harris became an American citizen in 1921 and the following year travelled to post-war Berlin where he began publishing, privately, the four volumes of biography/erotica for which he is most notorious. His descriptions of his alleged sexual encounters, highly graphic for the time and accompanied by illustrations that left nothing to the imagination, resulted in the book being widely banned. Inevitable comparisons were made with D. H. Lawrence's *Lady Chatterley's Lover*. In the US and Britain the ban lasted for over forty years. In addition to describing and probably greatly exaggerating his own sex life, he also discussed the nocturnal activities of, amongst others, Charles Stewart Parnell, Randolph Churchill and William E. Gladstone.

Harris numbered Oscar Wilde among his friends. He, sensibly, as it turned out, advised Wilde against suing the Marquis of Queensberry for defamation in the trial that destroyed the Irish playwright. Wilde had dedicated his play *An Ideal Husband* to

Harris. So ill-suited was Harris to that particular designation – he was married three times – that we might well assume the playwright had his tongue firmly in his cheek when he did so. Harris also wrote a not entirely favourable biography of Wilde. He died, in 1931, of a heart attack, at the age of seventy-five.

Frank Harris, cowboy, editor, biographer, and *bon vivant,* was born one hundred and fifty-eight years ago, on this day.

Broadcast 14 February 2014

27 February 1890
Danny Needham and Patsy Kerrigan
Fight a Draw in San Francisco

Perhaps the most celebrated boxer to come out of San Francisco was the son of an Irish emigrant. James J. Corbett, better known as Gentleman Jim, was born in 1866, fought twenty-four professional bouts and defeated the great John L. Sullivan to become World Heavyweight Champion. His father was from Mayo; his uncle, who shared his name, was a parish priest in the county.

But while Corbett may have been the greatest Irish-American boxing champion to emerge from the city, the greatest, and indeed the longest, fight involved another Irish-American, Danny Needham.

Needham was born in St Paul, Minnesota, a year after Corbett. He was one of four brothers who were constantly in trouble with the law until he found his natural home in the ring, fighting as a lightweight. The 1880s had seen the establishment of Queensberry rules, but professional boxing back then was very different to the sport as practised today. Most fighters wore two-ounce gloves – four-ounce gloves were scathingly referred to as 'pillows'. Today boxers wear gloves weighing 8-10 ounces. In most cases there was no limit to the number of three-minute rounds that could be fought. Boxers generally agreed to keep going until one or the other was knocked out or threw in the towel. The sport in America was dominated by men with names like Paddy Duffy, Dan Murphy, Charlie Gleason, Charlie 'Bull' McCarthy and Jack McGinty, as well as Sullivan and Corbett. It was a very Irish sport and a very Irish route out of poverty.

Danny Needham was a colourful character, to say the least. He had a reputation for petty theft when he wasn't in training and always carried a revolver with him. In 1890 he was persuaded by his manager to move up a division to welterweight and to try his luck in San Francisco. There he encountered the Scotch-Irish boxer Patsy Kerrigan. Needham was conceding six pounds to Kerrigan. The fight turned into an epic – the *War and Peace* of professional boxing – although there wasn't a whole lot of peace in evidence.

The bout began shortly after 8.30 p.m. in front of an enthusiastic crowd. It ended six hours and thirty-nine minutes later after one hundred rounds, the second longest bout in pugilistic history. The longest, one hundred and eleven rounds, came three years later between Andy Bowen and Jack Burke in New Orleans. According to one newspaper report, 'Needham was pushed down three times in the fifty-sixth round and four times in the seventieth, but he arose and fought on desperately'.

Neither boxer laid a glove on his opponent in the final eleven rounds, both were so exhausted they simply stalked each other around the ring, feinting from time to time. Eventually the referee called it a draw at 3.15 a.m. Some of the spectators had actually left the arena and returned a number of hours later to discover, to their surprise, that both fighters were still on their feet.

Later in life Needham went prospecting in Alaska, attempted to murder a man who had been stalking his wife and was jailed for armed robbery in 1899. He died at the age of fifty-five, having spent the last two years of his life in a mental institution.

Danny Needham and Patsy Kerrigan eventually fought each other to a standstill in San Francisco in one of only two boxing contests to go over one hundred rounds, one hundred and twenty-five years ago, on this day.

Broadcast 27 February 2015

21 February 1922
Recruitment Begins for
An Garda Síochána

An Garda Síochána are in the jobs market again. Although only two hundred and fifty trainees will be taken on, already there is no shortage of young men and women keen to join.

In the minds of the country's founding fathers in 1922, there was no doubt that one of the first colonial institutions to go would be the paramilitary Royal Irish Constabulary. The Dublin Metropolitan Police, an unarmed force, some of whose members had provided Michael Collins with valuable intelligence, was left intact for the time being. Among the agents of Collins was Ned Broy, who subsequently became Garda Commissioner – in the process making a remarkable recovery from having been murdered in Neil Jordan's *Michael Collins* movie. So the DMP, the less objectionable force, wasn't subsumed into the newly created An Garda Síochána until 1925.

New recruits had to sit an exam in reading, spelling and arithmetic. They had to be five foot nine inches tall and between nineteen and twenty-seven years of age to become cadets. The very first Civic Guard – the name originally chosen for the force – was, as it happens, an ex-RIC man, P. J. Kerrigan.

The second Garda Commissioner was the infamous Eoin O'Duffy, founder of the Blueshirts. O'Duffy was dismissed by the newly elected Fianna Fáil government in 1933. There have been nineteen Garda Commissioners to date.

Perhaps the most famous guard was the Dubliner Jim 'Lugs' Branigan who regularly used his fists, officially and unofficially, in the course of his duties. Branigan was in his pomp at the time of the so-called Animal Gangs in the 1930s and 40s. In May 1940, at the 'Battle of Baldoyle', Branigan (and other guards) were forced to wade in and disarm gang members equipped with bayonets, butchers knives, swords and razors. When challenged on their way to the confrontation, they had claimed to be going to a wedding. Injuries included a knife through the lung of one gang member and a rusty bayonet through the thigh of another. It appears that while there were plenty of grooms and best-men around, the bride never showed.

Branigan retired on 6 January 1973. He received many tributes, but was particularly touched by a canteen of cutlery and a set of Waterford Crystal glasses from a group of Dublin prostitutes who regarded him as something of a father figure.

According to the Garda Roll of Honour, a surprising eighty-six members of the force have died on active duty. While some deaths were accidental, many guards have been murdered since the force was established. One of the earliest was Henry Phelan, on 14 November 1922. Garda Phelan was killed by armed men when he went to a shop in Mullinahone, Co. Tipperary to purchase hurleys.

In 1970, in the early days of the Troubles in Northern Ireland, Garda Richard Fallon pursued armed members of the Republican splinter group Saor Éire and was fatally wounded when shot by one of the raiders. Two years later Inspector Samuel Donegan was conducting searches on the Cavan/Fermanagh border when he was killed by a booby-trap bomb in a country lane.

The Scott Medal, awarded to members of the Gardaí for bravery, has become something of a yardstick for troubled times in Ireland. In the 1970s, when paramilitary activity was at its height, there were ninety-six Scott Medals awarded. Contrast that with a total of six between 1951-60.

In an era when many of the bastions of Irish society have fallen into disrepute, An Garda Síochána has been no exception. The force has had dark periods of its own. While the 1970s may have seen almost one hundred Scott Medals, it was also the era of the so-called Heavy Gang. The release of the Morris Report in 2008, which delved into the corrupt and undisciplined activities of members of the force in Donegal made for embarrassing reading. The findings of the Smithwick Tribunal and the controversy over the 'wiping' of penalty points could well add some more unhappy chapters.

But by and large, the Garda Síochána, still, astonishingly, a mostly unarmed police force, has served the country well and remains one of the few national institutions that continues to command popular respect and admiration.

A recruitment drive for the Civic Guards began ninety-two years ago, on this day.

Broadcast 21 February 2014

7 February 1940
The Sentencing of IRA Activist
Brendan Behan

Brendan Behan was born in Dublin's inner city in 1923. He inherited his love of literature from his father, a house-painter who had fought in the War of Independence, and much of his republicanism from his mother Kathleen, a sister of Peadar Kearney, the man who wrote 'The Soldier's Song'.

Behan was politically active from an early age and was also publishing poetry as a teenager. He was one of the youngest contributors to the *Irish Press* with his poem, 'Reply of a Young Boy to pro-English Verses'.

At the age of sixteen he joined the IRA and decided, apparently of his own volition, that it would be a good idea to bomb the Liverpool docks. This resulted in his arrest in England for possession of explosives. His explanation to the court for the contents of the bag with which he was discovered was that the potassium chlorate found in his luggage was medication for his ears. He even claimed to have a doctor's note to that effect. The judge was not impressed. Pronouncing sentence, he told Behan that, but for his youth, his prison sentence would have been much longer. He was committed to a borstal for three years. On the very day that he was sent down, two IRA volunteers, Peter Barnes and William McCormick, were hanged in Winston Green prison in Birmingham for their involvement in an explosion that killed five people in Coventry in 1939. Behan's sojourn in prison would become the inspiration for his autobiographical novel *Borstal Boy*.

On his return to Ireland Behan was jailed once again and sentenced to fourteen years in prison for the attempted murder of two Irish detectives. He was released in a general amnesty in 1946. He maintained a healthy disrespect for the forces of law and order, once observing that, 'I have never seen a situation so dismal that a policeman couldn't make worse'. His militant republican activities had ended by his mid-twenties.

His first major commercial and artistic success was his prison play *The Quare Fellow*. This started life in the Pike Theatre in Dublin before the famous English director Joan Littlewood took it to London. The play was an instant success and was transferred to the West End. Behan did the cause of the play no particular harm, whatever about his own reputation, when he appeared drunk on a BBC TV interview with the rather self-important Malcolm Muggeridge. Sceptics, unwilling to accept Behan's credentials as a writer, claimed, unfairly, that it was really Littlewood who had crafted *The Quare Fellow*, prompting the gibe that 'While Dylan Thomas wrote *Under Milk Wood*, Brendan Behan wrote under Littlewood'.

Further success followed with *The Hostage* in 1958, an English-language version of his play *An Giall*, first produced in the Damer Theatre on Stephen's Green. Some claim that the resemblance between the two is a passing one. The appearance of *Borstal Boy* the same year further enhanced his growing reputation.

Unfortunately, Behan was, at this time, becoming almost as well known for his drinking as for his writing. He once described himself as a 'drinker with writing problems' and one *bon mot* ascribed to him on a visit to North America was the observation that 'I saw a billboard saying "Drink Canada Dry" – so I did'. Like another famous Celtic roisterer, the aforementioned Dylan

Thomas, Behan would have a short life. He developed diabetes in his thirties and it hastened his death. He collapsed in a Dublin bar in 1964 and died in hospital. He was only forty-one years old.

Brendan Behan, two days short of his seventeenth birthday, was sentenced to three years in borstal at Liverpool Assizes, seventy-four years ago, on this day.

Broadcast 7 February 2014

6 February 1958
The Death of Football Star Liam
Whelan in the Munich Air Disaster

You are probably unfamiliar with the name William Augustine Whelan. You may not even be familiar with the name by which he was better known, Liam or Billy Whelan. But he was, and still is, the great 'lost genius' of Irish football. He hated flying, which is ironic, because he is also one of Ireland's most celebrated air-crash victims.

Whelan was born on April Fool's Day 1935 and spent his footballing life making fools of many defenders, both amateur and professional alike. Like so many gifted young Irish footballers, he played for Home Farm, the great Dublin youth team. From there he progressed to the very top of the professional ranks when he was scouted and signed by Manchester United. He was one of the 'Busby Babes', playing in the position then known as 'inside forward' – today he would be an attacking midfielder. His boss was the great Scottish manager Matt Busby who, in the 1950s, was in the process of assembling a young squad and building Manchester United into one of the premier European sides.

Whelan might have expected to serve the sort of long rugged apprenticeship customary for young professional footballers in the 1950s. Lots of boot-cleaning and maintenance and the distant hope of making it to the top level. But he actually broke into the United first team at the age of eighteen. Two years later he was joined by another teenager, one Robert Charlton from Northumberland.

In his four seasons at Manchester United, Whelan made ninety-eight first team appearances. He averaged more than a goal every two games, scoring fifty-two in total for the club. He played four times for the Republic of Ireland but did not score. He was United's top goal scorer in the 1956/57 season when his team won the old First Division championship. With twenty-six goals in the League, Whelan contributed a quarter of United's tally that season.

In the 1957/58 season, as First Division champions, Manchester United became the first English club to play in the European Cup, a competition which had been, up to that point, dominated by Real Madrid, but was held in low esteem by the English Football Association. They reached the quarter-finals, where they beat the Yugoslav champions, Red Star Belgrade, the second leg of the tie taking place in Serbia. The flight they took back to England stopped off for re-fuelling in Munich. A direct Belgrade to Manchester flight was beyond the range of the Airspeed Ambassador plane in which the team travelled. While the passengers waited in the Munich terminal building, snow began to fall heavily. Two take-off attempts were aborted. The passengers were asked to disembark while minor repairs were carried out.

Just before the plane took off for the third time, Whelan was overheard by one of the other passengers to remark nervously and fatalistically to one of his teammates 'Well, if this is the time, then I'm ready'. Tragically, it was the time. The Airspeed Ambassador hit slush at the end of the runway, slowing the plane down. It did not now have sufficient speed to take off and skidded through a barrier, collided with a house and broke in two pieces. Of the forty-four passengers and crew, twenty-three died, including eight of the seventeen Manchester United players on board. Whelan was one of the fatalities.

In 2006 he had a railway bridge named after him in Cabra, not far from Dalymount Park, where he had played with the Irish international team. The unveiling was performed by his teammate and one of the fortunate survivors of the Munich Air disaster, Sir Bobby Charlton, another goal scoring inside-forward who lived to realise his potential with World and European Cup medals, one hundred and six caps for his country and the prized Ballon d'Or – world player of the year – in 1966. While Whelan would never have won a World Cup winners medal, all that Bobby Charlton had achieved would have been available to him.

Liam Whelan was two months shy of his twenty-third birthday when he died, fifty-seven years ago, on this day.

Broadcast 6 February 2015

March

Ars gratia artis

7 March 1594
The English Take on 'Pirate Queen' Grace O'Malley

Grace O'Malley, born in 1530, was from a seafaring family based around Clew Bay in Co. Mayo. Seafaring can be interpreted as a bit of a euphemism for piracy. Her family, with its main stronghold on Clare Island, reserved to itself the right to 'levy' all vessels fishing off their coastline, no matter where they came from. Whether that was tax collecting or piracy is a moot point. To this day there are those who still see little distinction between the two pursuits anyway.

The only child of Eoghan Dubhdara and Maeve O'Malley, Grace was a bit of a tomboy to say the least. She was flamboyant and belligerent and as a child she earned her famous nickname 'Granuaile' by cutting off her hair when her father refused to take her on an expedition to Spain on the spurious pretext that her long tresses might catch in the ship's rigging. Thereafter, she became known as 'Bald Grace' or Gráinne Mhaol.

She was married twice and was rumoured to have had many lovers, although this was an accusation regularly levelled against powerful women during the sixteenth century. Her first husband was Dónal an Chogaidh O'Flaherty – Donal of the Battles – whom she married at the age of sixteen. After his death Grace set her cap at the wealthy and influential Richard Bourke. He was known as

Risteárd an Iarainn (Richard of the Iron) either because he always insisted on wearing a coat of mail inherited from his Norman ancestors or because he controlled much of the iron manufacturing in Connacht. Or both.

Grace and Richard married under the Brehon Law, which, as it happened, allowed a wife to divorce her husband. And, as it happened, that appears to have been exactly what occurred. Grace, installed in Bourke's ancestral pile, Rockfleet Castle, ended the marriage by the simple device of telling her husband 'Richard Bourke, I dismiss you'. But she cleverly did not dismiss the Castle.

Grace and her first husband, Dónal O'Flaherty, didn't make themselves very popular with the merchants of Galway, who complained to the English court that the O'Malleys and the O'Flahertys were behaving like pirates. Not that Granuaile confined her activities to her own back yard of Galway. Her revenue-raising exercises ranged all along the south and west coasts.

She was, by and large, a supporter of rebellion, though she was not averse to helping out the English administration in Ireland when it suited her. This changed, however, when her sworn enemy, the English governor of Connacht, Richard Bingham, kidnapped two of her sons and her half-brother in 1593. Grace took the unusual step of sailing to England to make the case for their release directly to Queen Elizabeth herself. It was, by all accounts, a memorable occasion, with Grace dressed in the sixteenth-century equivalent of creations by John Rocha and Phillip Treacy. The essential difference was that she sported her own concealed dagger; *de rigueur* in the Tudor period, but something that would ruin the line of a piece of twenty-first century couture.

Elizabeth was impressed by the Irish Pirate Queen, politically empowered women being thin on the ground at the time. An accommodation was reached which didn't last very long and resulted in a fleet being despatched to seek and destroy Granuaile's power base. Between the time of her meeting with Elizabeth and her death, probably in 1603, Grace threw her support behind the forces gathered by O'Neill and O'Donnell in the Nine Years' War.

O'Malley has been fêted in prose, poetry and music by artists as diverse as Shaun Davey, Patrick Pearse and the Sawdoctors. The Commissioners of Irish Lights have named not one but three vessels after her, though the fact that the *Asgard* carried a figurehead of Grace didn't stop it sinking in 2008.

An English expedition prepared to leave Galway to take on the might of Grace O'Malley, aka Granuaile, aka the Pirate Queen, four hundred and twenty years ago, on this day.

Broadcast on 7 March 2014

21 March 1656
The Death of Philosopher and
Theologian James Ussher

In case you ever wondered about the date on which the universe was created, it was apparently 23 October 4004 BC. That may seem a trifle recent to many of us, given that the dinosaurs are reliably reported to have ruled the earth millions of years ago, but this was the carefully deduced calculation of the seventeenth-century Church of Ireland Archbishop of Armagh, James Ussher.

Ussher was born in 1581 into a wealthy Anglo-Irish family. He was one of the first students to attend Trinity College, Dublin. It was established in 1591, and he became a student there in 1594, at the tender age of thirteen. His callow youth would today result in him being rejected by the computer in the CAO application process, but going to college in your early teens was not that unusual in the sixteenth century. Ussher occupied the post of Professor of Theological Controversies there, which would be an extremely interesting position for a committed creationist today. Today, one of the college libraries in Trinity is named after him.

He became Primate of All Ireland in 1625 and occupied the position until his death in 1656 – so he served during interesting times. However, he left Ireland in 1640 for what turned out to be the last time. The rebellion of 1641 saw him lose his home and income at the hands of Catholic rebels.

Even before losing much of his personal wealth he wasn't really a fan of Roman Catholicism and was not in favour of allowing Catholics to exercise their religion freely. He once wrote that 'The religion of the papists is superstitious and idolatrous; their faith and doctrine erroneous and heretical'. So not much ecumenical wriggle room there. It may come as a surprise, therefore, to learn that Ussher's own mother was a Catholic.

During the English Civil War he was forced to choose sides. He chose the wrong one. Although something of a Puritan himself, he opted to remain loyal to King Charles. Only the protection of influential friends allowed him to remain unscathed in London after the victory of the Parliamentarians. From the roof of the Countess of Peterborough's house he watched the execution of the King, but is reported to have fainted before the axe fell.

It was in 1650, in *The Annals of the Old Testament*, that he published the result of his calculations as to the date of the creation of the world, a feat also attempted, by the way, by Isaac Newton. His rationale was that Christ had actually been born in 4 BC and that the world had been created precisely 4,000 years earlier, with God starting at sunset on 22 October and finishing the job the following day. As Solomon's temple had been built 1,000 years before the birth of Christ, and as it had been constructed 3,000 years *after* the act of creation, that meant 4,004 BC was the year of Genesis. He also claimed that Adam had been created at the same time. His theory is still popular with many who don't hold with the theory of evolution or the science of carbon-dating. Clarence Darrow raised Ussher's calculations in his cross-examination of William Jennings Bryan at the famous Scopes trial, the so-called 'Monkey trial' in 1925, where a teacher was prosecuted for teaching the theory of evolution to his students. Despite his support for King Charles in the Civil War, Ussher, possibly because of his latent Puritanism, was held in such high esteem that he was buried in Westminster Cathedral, with the approval of Oliver Cromwell.

James Ussher, bishop, theologian and philosopher, died three hundred and fifty-nine years ago, on this day.

Broadcast 21 March 2014

14 March 1738
John Beresford, Unionist Politician, is Born in Dublin

Beresford is a name that used to have quite a bit of clout in Waterford. The most prominent member of the household of that name, John Beresford, was born in 1738 and represented the county in the Irish parliament for nearly forty years, which was no mean achievement, even though his family pretty much 'owned' the constituency.

Born on the Abbeville Estate near Dublin, in more recent times home to an equally powerful Irish political magnate, one Charles J. Haughey, Beresford had a typically aristocratic education at Kilkenny College and Trinity College, Dublin.

His first wife, a French lady named Constantia Ligondes, died in 1772. Two years later he married the society beauty Barbara Montgomery, who had been one of the models for the famous painting, *Three Ladies Adorning a Term of Hymen,* or the *Three Graces,* by Sir Joshua Reynolds. It was a good career move, but not as good as hitching his wagon to the train of the Tory politician William Pitt (the Younger), twice Prime Minister of England.

Beresford wielded enormous power in Ireland from the relatively modest position of a seat on the board of the revenue commissioners. After his promotion to the position of first Commissioner of Revenue in 1780 – making him the eighteenth century equivalent of Josephine Feehily – he brought about a number of key reforms to make the collection of taxes more efficient and more lucrative for the government, for which, I'm sure, we're all very grateful.

Beresford also took an interest in the architecture and streetscapes of Dublin. It was due to his influence that the Custom House was built – it took ten years and cost £400,000 – and that Sackville St. and the Quays were widened and extended.

When William Pitt became Prime Minister of Britain in 1783 Beresford's influence on Irish affairs, already huge, became even greater. He was, however, courteously loathed by the so-called 'Patriots', led by Henry Grattan in the Irish parliament, who had extracted major concessions on a very basic form of Home Rule from the British government in 1782. The feeling was mutual, by the way.

When, in 1795, that government made an even greater concession to Grattan and his followers by sending the conciliatory Earl Fitzwilliam over to Dublin as Lord Lieutenant, the beacon fires of warning were lit on the Beresford estates in Waterford. Fitzwilliam, finding that he could not operate in government without the approval of Beresford, rapidly fired him. Although he left him in possession of his salary of £2,000 a year, it was not a clever move. Beresford whined to William Pitt and Fitzwilliam himself was quickly fired in turn.

Sometime later, comments made by Fitzwilliam about Beresford being guilty of 'maladminstration' resulted in the Irish politician challenging the English earl to a duel. The two were due to meet in Kensington, where today such encounters take place over the bargain bin in Harrods. Fortunately the authorities got there first and the duel was abandoned. Beresford's honour was restored when Fitzwilliam agreed to apologise.

Beresford was, at first, opposed to the Act of Union, but, like a number of Irish notables, allowed himself to be cajoled into the belief that it was a very good idea. There is, of course, no suggestion that any money changed hands in persuading him to abandon his opposition. Catholic Emancipation, however, which was supposed to be introduced at the same time, was a bridge too far. Beresford was utterly opposed to Catholics obtaining any more rights and privileges than they had already acquired. His joy was unconfined when the King agreed and refused to allow Pitt to legislate for the entry of Catholics into Parliament.

So it was fitting that it was a Beresford – George – whose defeat by an emancipation candidate in the Waterford by-election of 1826 paved the way for Daniel O'Connell to win a seat in Clare two years later. By then John Beresford had gone to his final reward, collecting revenues in the next world.

John Beresford, landowner, politician, intriguer and tax collector was born two hundred and seventy-six years ago, on this day.

Broadcast on 14 March 2014

28 March 1820
The Birth of *Times* War
Correspondent William Howard
Russell

A certain Lt. Charles Naysmith can probably be said to be the father of professional war journalism ... by default. He was an officer with the East India Company's Bombay Artillery and was meant to be sending reports on the war in the Crimea to the *Times* in London. However, he lacked one great quality of any decent newsman, a sense of urgency. So the newspaper of record decided to send one of its own instead, an Irishman from Tallaght in Co. Dublin and a graduate of Trinity College, William Howard Russell. Russell was not sent, as is often the case, because as an Irishman he was more expendable, but because he was already near the top of his profession.

Russell's reporting from the bungled war in the Crimea aroused the ire of, among others, Prince Albert. Queen Victoria's consort wrote of Russell that 'the pen and ink of one miserable scribbler is despoiling the country'. So we have to assume that he was doing something right. The myth of Russell is that he was a campaigning polemicist who exposed the incompetence of the British High Command and whose blistering indictment of the army's derisory medical facilities, which were killing far more ordinary soldiers than the Russians, led to the arrival of Florence Nightingale in the

Crimea. This resulted in the consequent increase in the average life expectancy of the average soldier and the birth of a caring legend. As with most myths, some of it is actually true.

Disease and abysmally inadequate hygiene were indeed far greater killers than Russian cannon or musketry in the Crimea. But it was not Russell who brought this to the attention of the readers of the *Times*. It was the paper's Constantinople correspondent, Thomas Cheney. Neither was Russell the only correspondent in the Crimea. He faced competition from his equally accomplished but much younger fellow Irishman Edwin Godkin of the Liberal London newspaper *The Daily News*.

Russell, however, was hugely influential in turning public opinion against the conduct of the Crimean campaign. He spent almost two years covering the war, but most of his published work tended to emphasise the qualities of bravery and valour displayed by the soldiers rather than the muddle headed, in-bred, casual incompetence of their generals. When describing one of the most catastrophic disasters in what was a regular downpour of military ineptitude, the infamous Charge of the Light Brigade, Russell wrote in a florid and heroic style worthy of 'The Battle of Maldon':

> The first line is broken, it is joined by the second, they never halt or check their speed an instant ... with a halo of flashing steel above their heads, and with a cheer that was many a noble fellow's death cry, they flew into the smoke of the batteries ...

It was an era of romanticism, so mundane and meaningless death was not permitted, not even to readers of the *Times*. Alfred, Lord Tennyson, duly took note, and futile gesture became enduring myth in one of his most famous poems, 'The Charge of the Light Brigade'.

But the salient part of Russell's own myth is true. He did make a difference. He was subjecting military incompetence to independent scrutiny for the first time. He had commendable moral courage because he had to put up with the hostility of many of the members of the officer corps. He was blacklisted for his journalism, and Lord Raglan, the British commander, advised his officers to have nothing to do with Russell. Furthermore, he established the campaigning credentials of the *Times* – earning the newspaper its nickname 'The Thunderer'. He set a standard in war reporting that was, for example, in stark contrast to the abysmal record of the journalists of the Great War.

William Howard Russell, the acknowledged father of war correspondence, a term, incidentally, which he loathed, was born in Tallaght, Co. Dublin, one hundred and ninety-four years ago, on this day.

Broadcast on 28 March 2014

6 March 1831
The Birth of Irish-American General
Philip Sheridan

The precise origins of the man who is supposed to have uttered the decidedly non-PC comment 'the only good Indian I ever saw was a dead Indian' are decidedly hazy. Was he born in Killinkere, Co. Cavan, during a trans-Atlantic voyage on an emigrant boat to the Americas, or in the USA itself? No one knows exactly, but no one totally trusts Phillip Sheridan's own version, which is that he was one hundred per cent American, born in Albany, New York.

Sheridan, while an immensely successful general, was a man of small stature. Because he never exceeded five feet five inches in height, he was known all his life as 'Little Phil'. Abraham Lincoln, who towered over Sheridan, once described him as 'a brown, chunky little chap, with a long body, short legs, not enough neck to hang him, and such long arms that if his ankles itch he can scratch them without stooping'.

Sheridan first made a name for himself at Westpoint Military Academy where he was suspended for a year for fighting with a classmate whom he had threatened to run through with a bayonet. This type of behaviour was apparently not encouraged by the authorities, despite the fact that he was training for an occupation in which he would be required to kill people.

His reputation was greatly enhanced in the American Civil War where, before his first major promotion to Brigadier General, he was described by his divisional commander as being 'worth his weight in gold' as a cavalry officer. Later on, his pursuit of Robert E. Lee's

Confederate army in the final campaign of the conflict forced the southern commander to seek surrender terms and end the war.

Two years later Sheridan headed west to begin the work for which he would become famous, or notorious, depending on your point of view: defending the area between the Mississippi river and the Rocky mountains from Native American nations like the Lakota and Cheyenne, who had lived on the Great Plains for centuries before the arrival of the white man.

His methods were utterly ruthless. Intent on corralling the Plains' tribes in Federal reservations, he encouraged white hunters to wipe out their main food supply, the buffalo. He was also General George Armstrong Custer's boss – not that Custer was much of a one for following orders if they got in the way of 'glorious triumphs'. This is exemplified in the Lakota settlement massacre on the Washita River in 1868, an atrocity that took place on Sheridan's watch. Given Custer's periodic unruliness, Sheridan might not have been all that traumatised when his egotistical subordinate came to a bad end at the hands of the Lakota and Cheyenne in 1876 at the Little Bighorn.

Sheridan was rewarded for his ruthless suppression of the various Indian insurgencies in the 1860s and 1870s when he was given command of the entire US Army and succeeded the legendary William Tecumseh Sherman in 1883.

He may never actually have used the words 'the only good Indian I ever saw was a dead Indian'. As a young man he is even reported to have had a child by a Native American woman with whom he had a lengthy relationship. He probably did say something approximating the most memorable statement attributed to him, but he always denied having uttered that telling phrase.

Philip Sheridan was born in Killinkere, Co. Cavan, on a trans-Atlantic passage to America, or in Albany, New York, one hundred and eighty-four years ago, on this day.

Broadcast 6 March 2015

27 March 1839
The Birth of John Ballance,
Prime Minister of New Zealand

If I told you that an Irish Prime Minister was born in 1839, you would doubtless respond, correctly, by pointing out that a) we don't have a Prime Minister we have a Taoiseach, and b) that anyone born in Ireland in 1839 would have spent their entire working life as a citizen of the United Kingdom of Great Britain and Ireland, of which the nearest thing to an Irish Prime Minister was the Duke of Wellington.

Except, of course, that John Ballance, born in Co. Antrim in 1839, went on to become the fourteenth Prime Minister of New Zealand. Born into farming stock, Ballance wanted to do anything but farm, and so left for Belfast at the age of eighteen. From there he migrated to Britain, working in the ironmongery business in Birmingham. At the age of twenty-four he married Miss Frances Taylor and migrated to New Zealand in 1866 for the betterment of her health. The move had little effect as, tragically, she died two years later.

An educated and bookish man, he indulged his literary side by establishing a newspaper, the *Herald*, in the town of Wanganui, where the couple settled. While participating in a military campaign in 1867 against a local Maori uprising he criticised the conduct of the same campaign in his newspaper – obviously a man of independent views.

From campaigning journalism he moved inexorably into politics – elected for Wanganui from 1879 as an Independent he quickly entered the New Zealand Cabinet as Minister for Customs and then Minister for Education. Ballance had witnessed religious riots in Belfast and that spectacle turned him into a life-long secularist. He inherited his politics from his mother, a Quaker, and went on to found the New Zealand Liberal Party – the first organised political party in that country.

In 1881 he lost his seat by four votes after a carriage containing seven of his supporters broke down and they were unable to cast their ballots. Re-elected in 1884 he held three further ministerial positions until the government he supported fell. In 1889 he became leader of the opposition and in 1890, after a successful election campaign, he became Prime Minister at the head of a Liberal Party government.

Ballance was responsible for introducing highly progressive systems of income and property tax and under his leadership, the New Zealand economy expanded. He also cultivated good relations with the country's Maori population, settling a lot of their nagging land issues. He was also responsible for the introduction of female suffrage – New Zealand was the first country in the world to allow women to vote.

He was at the height of his powers and popularity in 1893 when, tragically, he died after an operation for an intestinal ailment at the age of fifty-four. Ballance has been described as 'unassuming and unpretentious' in style and as a quiet, polite, and patient man. How he ended up as a politician, therefore, is a complete mystery.

John Ballance, the Antrim-born fourteenth Prime Minister of New Zealand, was born, one hundred and seventy-six years ago, on this day.

Broadcast on 27 March 2015

13 March 1856
The Birth of Nationalist and Fenian
P. W. Nally

In September 2003 the redevelopment of Croke Park led to the demolition of the old Nally Stand and the creation of the Nally Terrace, adjacent to Hill 16. While people would be well aware that the stadium's Hogan Stand was called after one of the victims of the unwelcome British visitors to Croke Park in November 1920, on Bloody Sunday, and that the Cusack Stand was named in honour of one of the GAA's founders, how many people would know the story behind the man for whom the old Nally Stand was dedicated in 1952?

Patrick W. Nally, as you might expect, was one of the motive forces behind the creation of the GAA in 1884, though for reasons that will become clear, he was not present at the pivotal meeting in Thurles that established the new body. He was a well-known athlete who began discussions with Michael Cusack in the 1870s about forming an organisation devoted to the promotion of Gaelic Games.

His motives, however, were not entirely sporting in nature. Nally was, at the time, a member of the Supreme Council of the revolutionary nationalist organisation the Irish Republican Brotherhood, which he had joined in his early twenties. He managed to keep his republican activities – his job was to import firearms into Connaught – secret from the local Mayo RIC by condemning agrarian outrages. This was, somewhat surprisingly, perfectly consistent with IRB policy. So much so that when he applied for a gun licence, the local RIC Inspector advised his superiors that it was safe to grant the request, asserting that Nally 'would lead a useful and loyal life'. Indeed he did, but not quite in the way the senior policeman anticipated.

With the Land War raging in 1880, Nally's IRB activities came to the attention of spymasters in Dublin Castle and London. To avoid arrest he left the country for two years, eventually returning in 1882. He was arrested on conspiracy to murder charges the following year – this was a favoured Dublin Castle ploy for jailing people it didn't much approve of. He was implicated by an informer, another common procedure at the time. Nally was convicted, and sentenced to ten years' penal servitude.

Halfway through his sentence, his father, W. R. Nally, sought assistance from an apparently unlikely source, Captain William O'Shea, husband of Katharine and later Parnell's nemesis. However, O'Shea, though a conservative nationalist and a bona fide charlatan, was a political opportunist with a history of murky associations with the IRB. O'Shea's self-serving efforts to secure Nally's early release came to nothing.

Nally did not, in the end, actually serve his full term. But that was only because he died, aged thirty-six, in Mountjoy Prison, days before he was due to be released in November 1891. Efforts had been made by Dublin Castle, with a promise of clemency and other rewards, to get him to implicate Charles Stewart Parnell in the organisation and encouragement of agrarian crimes at a Special Commission of Inquiry which was tasked with investigating such allegations. He is said to have responded to these blandishments by insisting that 'not all the gold or honours that the Queen could bestow would induce Patrick Nally to become a traitor'.

The official cause of Nally's death was typhoid fever – some, however, suspected foul play. A Dublin coroner's jury held that his 'naturally strong constitution' had been broken by 'the harsh and cruel treatment to which he was subjected ... for refusing to give evidence ... at the Special Commission'. He was pre-deceased by four weeks by the man he had refused to betray to secure his release. At his funeral the same green flag was draped over Nally's coffin as had enveloped that of Parnell a month before.

Patrick W. Nally, revolutionary nationalist and sportsman, was born one hundred and fifty-nine years ago, on this day.

Broadcast 13 March 2015

20 March 1919
The Birth of the MGM Lion, Cairbre, in Dublin Zoo

They used to boast that they had 'more stars than there are in the heavens', though their official motto was the lofty *ars gratia artis* – which translates from bog Latin as 'art for art's sake'. Their first mascot was re-named Slats and was succeeded by, among others, Jackie, Tanner, George and Leo.

What am I talking about? This! [Roar of a lion.]

The boastful organisation told not a word of a lie – MGM in the 1930s and 40s had some of the biggest names in Hollywood under contract, with stars like Clark Gable, Joan Crawford, Greta Garbo, Judy Garland, Gene Kelly, Fred Astaire – need I go on? As regards the motto, don't believe a word of it – it was art all right, but it was purely for the sake of money.

The logo was a different matter entirely. When Samuel Goldwyn's old studio, Goldwyn Pictures, merged with the exhibition business Metro and Louis B. Mayer Pictures in 1924, the Goldwyn company had already started using a lion in their pre-credit sequence. MGM decided to continue the practice, and the first occasion on which the MGM lion appeared before one of the studio's movies was in the utterly forgettable and accordingly utterly forgotten *He Who Gets Slapped*, a silent movie starring Lon Chaney and Norma Shearer. Perhaps it's a 1920s version of *Fifty Shades of Grey*, but who knows?

And what has all this got to do with us, I hear you say?

Well, it's because of the identity of the very first MGM lion. The studio called him Slats, but that wasn't his real name. It was Cairbre. And he wasn't African or even Californian, he was a genuine

Dub. Cairbre was born in Dublin Zoo in 1919 and was named after Cúchulainn's charioteer, or a High King of Ireland, or a rebellious pretender to the High Kingship, or whatever you're having yourself.

Cairbre had, apparently, been introduced to Sam Goldwyn and the silver screen by fellow Dub Cedric Gibbons, the designer and art director. He also designed the statuette to be presented to members of the Academy of Motion Picture Arts and Sciences at their annual award ceremony. We know them more familiarly today as the Oscars. Gibbons apparently modelled the statuette on his wife, the statuesque film star Dolores del Rio. This means that Gibbons is personally responsible for two enduring Hollywood icons, neither of them human.

But back to Cairbre. There is a famous photograph of two men filming him for the MGM logo. Health and Safety considerations don't seem to have been paramount (no pun intended – though, ironically, that's where the shoot took place – Paramount Studios). Camera crew and big cat are separated, not by a hefty iron grille, but by a few feet of clear air. Were Cairbre of malevolent disposition he could have had a snack of cinematographer sushi any time he wanted.

Cairbre's image continued to be used on all the old black and white, silent MGM movies until 1928. As no one had recorded his heavily Dublin-accented roar, when the talkies began he was replaced by the more garrulous Jackie. He died at the age of seventeen and although his hide is on display in a museum in Kansas, he should not be confused with the cowardly lion of MGM's *The Wizard of Oz*.

When the comedian Mary Tyler Moore formed her own production company MTM in the 1960s – she mimicked the MGM logo, but replaced Cairbre with a little pussycat – it's highly unlikely the kitty is also Irish.

Cairbre, the big cat who tossed his mane from side to side for MGM, was born ninety-six years ago, on this day.

Broadcast 20 March 2015

April

Count Redmond O'Hanlon, the gallant rapparee

25 April 1681
The Murder of the Notorious Bandit Redmond O'Hanlon

Nowadays, a Tory is someone who sits on the government benches at Westminster. But three hundred years ago, before the term acquired its political connotation, a Tory was a different class of bandit entirely.

> *There was a man lived in the north, a hero brave and bold*
> *Who robbed the wealthy landlords of their silver and their gold*
> *He gave the money to the poor, to pay their rent and fee*
> *For Count Redmond O'Hanlon was a gallant rapparee.*

Thus begins Tommy Makem's account of one of the most illustrious and iconic thieves in seventeenth-century Ireland, Redmond O'Hanlon, the infamous Tory, highwayman, raparree and highway robber. Over the years O'Hanlon has acquired the characteristics of a Robin Hood and a Michael Dwyer – a fervent nationalist who believed in the re-distribution of wealth – other people's. He was, of course, neither a nationalist nor a socialist – the concepts being entirely unknown when he was in his pomp.

O'Hanlon, whose family had been wealthy Gaelic landowners before the intervention of Oliver Cromwell and others, was probably born in the vicinity of Slieve Gullion in South Armagh, and probably in the vicinity of 1640. Like so many members of the old Irish-Catholic nobility, he saw service in the army of the King of France and returned to Ireland at the time of the restoration of King Charles II to the English throne. The resumption of the monarchy led to no similar improvement in the fortunes of the O'Hanlon clan, so Redmond took to the hills to earn his living off the fortunes of those he saw as having dispossessed his family, viz. the Anglo-Irish nobility.

His operation was rather more sophisticated than simply standing in the middle of what passed for seventeenth-century roads and hollering 'Stand and deliver, your money or your life' in the style of Adam Ant. He made quite a good living from a primitive protection racket – those who paid him off were to be immune from the depredations of any of the raparees in his North Louth-South Armagh bailiwick. Should the local Tories baulk at Redmond's racket there was a simple 'three strikes and you're out' policy. Anyone caught robbing one of O'Hanlon's protectees was first warned off, thereafter they were fined for a second offence, and finally, if they did it again, they were murdered.

Naturally enough, the authorities disapproved of this primitive *pax Redmondica,* or perhaps *tax Redmondica* is more appropriate, and sent troops after him to pierce his protective mantle. O'Hanlon used a number of wily evasion techniques to elude capture, the most celebrated being the practice of reversing his horse's shoes to send his pursuers in the wrong direction. He was also known to reverse his and his accomplices' clothing to cause further confusion.

An inability to track Redmond resulted in the price on his head being raised consistently and repeatedly, leading to open season for a new breed of opportunist, the 'Tory hunter'. This was a similar animal to the more recent Wild West bounty hunter except six thousand miles to the east, two centuries earlier and with an Irish accent. When not pursuing Redmond with a view to claiming the considerable reward on his head, planter families like the Cootes of

Cootehill in Co. Cavan kept their hands in by hunting and killing Catholic priests.

Predictably, the death of Redmond was an inside job. He was betrayed and shot by a kinsman, Art McCall O'Hanlon, who was in it for the reward. *Pour encourager les autres,* Redmond's head was placed on a spike outside Downpatrick jail after Art imitated nature and succumbed to the blandishment of piles of money.

Redmond O'Hanlon, Tory, raparee, extortionist and folk hero, died three hundred and thirty-three years ago, on this day.

Broadcast 25 April 2014

18 April 1690
The First of the 'Wild Geese' Sail for France

When Ireland play France in rugby in Dublin every two years, it's usually an opportunity for thousands of French rugby supporters to fly from Paris and other parts of France to support their team. To ensure that the planes don't return empty, many Irish tourists – presumably *not* rugby supporters – take advantage of heavily discounted fares to spend a few days in France.

This is something akin to what happened in April 1690 when five thousand Irish soldiers sailed from Ireland to France on the ships that had bought six thousand French soldiers in the opposite direction.

Louis XIV of France – the famous Sun King – was conducting a war in Holland but had still offered support to the recently supplanted English King, James II, in his struggle with William of Orange for the throne of England. Louis was willing to send French troops to Ireland to assist the cause of the Catholic King James (whose alliance with France, incidentally, made him an enemy of the Vatican – which meant that King Billy and the Pope were actually on the same side in the Williamite Wars). However, the Sun King was not prepared to forego six thousand men in his fight with the Dutch so he demanded an equivalent number of Irish troops to replace his own men sailing to Ireland.

Why did Louis not just hang on to his own soldiers rather than making a direct swop? A very good question. The answer will be found in the footnotes at the end of this piece. If you can find the footnotes. The five thousand Irishmen became the basis for the

Irish Brigades who fought in the French army for the next century.

This first detachment of the so-called 'Wild Geese' was led by Justin McCarthy (aka Lord Mountcashel), Daniel O'Brien and Arthur Dillon. After the Treaty of Limerick, signed in 1691, and the collapse of the resistance of the Jacobite forces in Ireland, they were joined by the celebrated Irish general, Patrick Sarsfield, the Earl of Lucan.

McCarthy was a charismatic individual who had been brought up in France when his father, Donough McCarthy, had left Ireland in the 1650's. Donough had incurred the wrath of Oliver Cromwell and it would have been unhealthy for him to remain in the country. The confiscated McCarthy estates were returned after the restoration of the Crown in England. However, when the infamous Titus Oates accused numerous Catholic peers of plotting to murder King Charles II, Mountcashel emulated his father and returned to the safety of France, which was a wise decision on his part. More than twenty alleged conspirators were executed before Oates was found guilty of perjury. Although Mountcashel commanded the Irish Brigade, his service to the French King was hampered by chronically bad eyesight and a wound received while fighting in the South of France. He died in 1694.

Patrick Sarsfield, created Earl of Lucan by King James when it was too late to derive much benefit from it, had an even shorter career on the continent. Sarsfield had distinguished himself in the Jacobite Wars as one of the best generals in the army assembled on behalf of King James. He was, accordingly, commissioned as a Lieutenant General in the army of King Louis and sent to fight in Flanders. There he died of his wounds after the Battle of Landen in 1693. More than a century and a half later, his great-great-great-great grandson, Michael Corcoran, would lead another Irish Brigade, this one serving in the Union army in the American Civil War.

The first 'Wild Geese', a force of five thousand Irish Jacobite soldiers, sailed for France three hundred and twenty-four years ago, on this day.

Broadcast 18 April 2014

4 April 1818
The Birth of Thomas Mayne Reid, Novelist of the American West

Born in 1818, and a native of Ballyroney, Co. Down, Thomas Mayne Reid was an adventurer before he became a highly successful writer. His father, a Presbyterian minister, intended him for the Church, but like a lot of sons Reid had ideas of his own. Despite spending four years training to be a minister he failed to graduate and did not follow in his father's footsteps.

He entered the USA via New Orleans in 1840 and quickly became involved in the activities of hunters and fur traders. He lasted six months in Louisiana and was, so the story goes, forced to leave the state for refusing to horsewhip a slave. He later set one of his books, the anti-slavery novel *The Quadroon*, in the South. While living in his next port of call, Philadelphia, and working as a journalist, he became a drinking companion of Edgar Allen Poe. The great American mystery writer later remarked of the Irishman's conversational talents that he was 'a colossal but most picturesque liar. He fibs on a surprising scale but with the finish of an artist'.

Reid fought in the Mexican–American War where he was double-jobbing as he was also covering the conflict for a New York newspaper as its war correspondent. He was badly wounded at the Battle of Chapultepec, where the Mexican defenders of the town included members of the famous San Patricio battalion, a group of Catholic Irishmen fed up with American nativist anti-Catholicism who had switched sides to fight with Mexico. Reid was promoted while most of the surviving San Patricios were hanged.

After spending just over a decade in the USA, mostly in the West, he returned to Europe and began to harvest his American experience as a writer. There is, however, scant evidence that he ever actually spent a lot of time in the part of the world where much of his work is located, the American West. Between 1848 and his death in 1883 he wrote more than seventy adventure novels and, ironically, as an Irishman writing mostly in Britain, played a huge part in the mythologising of the West, even amongst Americans. Theodore Roosevelt was an avid fan of Reid's novels as a young boy and later went in search of the West that Reid wrote about. If he didn't actually find it he certainly pretended to.

Reid cultivated a rather foppish appearance. He liked to wear lemon-yellow gloves as well as clothes that were guaranteed to attract attention. He also wore a monocle, giving rise to the myth that he had a glass eye. The story is told that when Reid and some other authors once met for a drink, the Irishman's glass eye fell into his beverage and had to be fished out.

The thrust of his approach to the West can be gauged from the titles of some of his more famous novels, many of which did not actually appear in American editions until well after his death. *The Scalp Hunters,* written in 1851, was one of his earliest and most successful efforts. Other classic 'dime novels' included *The Headless Horseman,* written in 1866, later read enthusiastically in a Russian translation by a young Vladimir Nabokov. It doesn't, however, appear to have greatly influenced the writing of *Lolita.* In all, Reid wrote seventy-five novels as well as numerous short stories.

Thomas Mayne Reid, novelist and teller of tall tales, was born one hundred and ninety-six years ago, on this day.

Broadcast 4 April 2014

3 April 1846
The Death of Street Balladeer
Michael Moran, a.k.a. Zozimus

The city of Dublin is supposed to be full of 'characters' – people you would go out of your way to meet and who will hold forth and entertain you at the drop of a wallet.

Whether the city deserves such a reputation is a moot point, but most will concede that one Michael Moran, probably born in 1794, was indeed a 'character'. Better known to us as Zozimus, he was a street balladeer who earned his living from writing and reciting his own poetry and ballads. He did so at a time when the street balladeer was a familiar sight in the city.

Moran, who became blind shortly after birth, had a phenomenal memory and took his stage or 'street' name from a fifth-century holy man, Zozimus of Palestine. He was born in the wonderfully named Faddle Alley near Blackpitts in the Liberties. He travelled the city in 'a long frieze coat, a greasy brown beaver hat, corduroy trousers' and a good pair of brogues. He was also rarely seen without a large blackthorn stick. While he ranged all over the city, his favourite haunt, where he would deliver his rhymes and recitations, was near what was then called Carlisle Bridge, now O'Connell Street Bridge.

One of his most celebrated verses is his song of praise for poteen:

> *Oh long life to the man who invented poteen –*
> *Sure the Pope ought to make him a martyr –*
> *If myself was this moment Victoria, the Queen,*
> *I'd drink nothing but whiskey and wather.*

Even in the first half of the eighteenth century street performers were constantly being 'moved on' or hassled by the constabulary. One Dublin Metropolitan policeman in particular – number 184B – had a set against Zozimus. This guardian of the law, however, went too far when he also began harassing a journalist named Dunphy. To this day sane citizens know that you don't mess with journalists by the name of Dunphy. The *Freeman's Journal* writer and the street poet conspired to make the policeman's life a misery. Zozimus wrote and regularly recited a verse which went:

> *How proud Robert Peel must be of such a chap*
> *He stands about five feet nothing in his cap*
> *And his name's immortalised by me friend MrD*
> *A statue must be riz to 184B*

Constable 184B subsequently became such an object of scorn on the streets of Dublin that he was forced to resign and, legend has it, his number was retired by the DMP as no one else would take it on.

Zozimus was obsessed with grave robbers and before his death, at around the age of fifty-five, asked that he be buried in the well-protected Glasnevin Cemetery. He wrote this verse to his friend Stoney Pockets:

> *Oh Stoney, Stoney*
> *Don't let the Sack-'em-Ups get me*
> *Send round the hat*
> *And buy me a grave.*

He got his wish, albeit in unmarked form, in a pauper's plot not far from Daniel O'Connell's more elaborate resting place in the shadow of a round tower. Since the 1960s a memorial marks his final resting place.

Michael Moran, better known as Zozimus, died one hundred and sixty-nine years ago, on this day.

Broadcast 3 April 2015

11 April 1866
The Last Successful Fenian Invasion of Canada

Between 1866 and 1871 American Fenians – mostly veterans of the Civil War – attempted, on no less than five occasions, to invade Canada with some nebulous idea of seizing what was known at the time as British North America. The plan was to return the territory only when Ireland was officially recognised as an independent republic.

Most of their efforts were cack-handed and disorganised. The raid on Campobello Island, New Brunswick, in April 1866 is typical. Led by one of the founders of the movement, John O'Mahony, this attempt landed seven hundred Fenians on the Canadian island that adjoined the state of Maine. However, the small force sensibly placed discretion ahead of valour when it was informed that British warships were on their way. The occupation of the island was painlessly brief.

Another raid in 1870 was betrayed by the most famous English spy in the American Fenian ranks, Thomas Beach, who posed for many years as a French-Canadian dentist, Henri le Caron. His information ensured that the British and Canadian authorities were well-aware of what the Fenians were up to.

The Fenian raids are generally represented as pathetic and disorganised fiascos. This is true of four out of the five – but not of the second raid, in June 1866.

The plan for this incursion was put together by former Union General Thomas William Sweeny, a Corkman known as 'Fighting Tom'. The force, of over one thousand Fenians, was led by former Union army Colonel John O'Neill. It managed to cross the Niagra River without any American interference. A US gunboat – the *Michigan* – should have stopped them. But it had been sabotaged by a Fenian member of its crew and didn't crank up until fourteen hours after most of the Fenian rebels had already made the crossing.

O'Neill's men defeated a Canadian militia force at the Battle of Ridgeway. The Canadian defenders were boys before men – they were mostly inexperienced and badly-armed troops facing well-equipped Irish veterans of the American Civil War. The result was the first Irish victory against a British force since Fontenoy in 1745.

The following day that first success was repeated at Fort Erie, a lakeside stronghold described by the *New York Times* as a 'deserted dunghill'. The *Times* was just as complimentary towards the Fenian force itself, describing its members as 'heroes of the stamp who bravely led the retreat at Bull Run'. The paper then advised the British-Canadian forces 'not to spare them on our account. They would be lying and stealing here if they were not raiding there'.

The Fenians described themselves as the Irish Republican Army – some went into battle wearing uniforms bearing the legend 'IRA' – it was the first time the letters are known to have been used in a context other than that of the accumulation of an American pension fund.

The USS *Michigan* finally managed to extract the Irish spanner from its works and it stopped Fenian reinforcements crossing into Canada. Rather than wait for the arrival of a vastly superior British regular force, O'Neill withdrew and evacuated his men by barge back across the Niagra to Buffalo. There the Fenians surrendered to US forces. A little known fact: included among the Irish invaders was a small force of Mohawk Indians and a smaller group of Black Civil War veterans.

In an attempt to prevent a recurrence, the US army was instructed to arrest anyone 'who looked like a Fenian'. This raised the obvious question, what does a Fenian look like? The Americans took the whole affair very seriously indeed. General Sweeny, the Civil War hero, was arrested for his part in the invasion. Oddly enough, he continued to serve in the US army until he retired in 1870. Or maybe that was his punishment.

One effect the raid did have was that it hastened the formation of the Confederation of Canada – so the Fenians can, in a sense, claim to be Canada's Founding Fathers.

In a far less successful incursion two months beforehand, Fenian forces, led by John O'Mahony, briefly occupied Campobello Island, New Brunswick, one hundred and forty-eight years ago, on this day.

Broadcast 11 April 2014

24 April 1916
The Easter Rising Begins in Dublin

As down the glen one Easter morn to a city fair rode I
There Armed lines of marching men in squadrons passed me by
No fife did hum nor battle drum did sound it's dread tattoo
But the Angelus bell o'er the Liffey swell rang out through the
foggy dew.

So begins the best-known song written about the 1916 Rising, 'The Foggy Dew', a song explicitly critical of those who opted to fight in the First World War rather than in Dublin.

Easter was late that year – only a week shy of May. The small rump of the Irish Volunteers, not much more than 10,000 strong, who had opposed John Redmond when he advocated enlistment in the British Army had scheduled manoeuvres for Easter Sunday.

What the supposed leader of the Volunteers, Prof. Eoin MacNeill, did not realise was that a small Irish Republican Brotherhood coterie within the Volunteers, indeed a small coterie within the larger IRB, planned to turn Easter Sunday training into a full-scale rebellion in major urban centres around the country. When MacNeill did find out, in the wake of an abortive attempt to bring in German weapons, he issued an order cancelling Volunteer activities on Sunday 23 April.

As every schoolchild knows, the infamous 'countermanding order' did not stop the Easter Rising from going ahead, but merely sowed confusion in the ranks and greatly reduced the turnout of Volunteers the following day when the insurrection actually began.

The first act of the rebels after taking the GPO was the reading of the Proclamation of the Irish Republic. It was not read from the steps of the GPO because the building then, as now, doesn't have steps. In fact, it may not even have been read by Patrick Pearse. There has been a suggestion that it was read by Thomas Clarke, the most senior IRB member among the seven signatories. Pearse, however, wins out on the balance of probability.

One of the more bizarre incidents of a week in which much of the centre of Dublin was burned was the arrival of two Swedish sailors at the door of the GPO. The two were offering their assistance to the Irish revolution – as long as it was over by Thursday when their ship was leaving Dublin port. Their generous offer was politely declined. Another slightly bizarre incident concerned an irritating British soldier who had been taken prisoner when the GPO was occupied. At some point during the week he managed to get hold of a bottle of whiskey and become blindingly drunk and even more irritating.

The odds against the success of the Easter Rising, prohibitive enough to begin with, were shortened by the failure to take Dublin Castle, the telephone exchange at Crow Street and to even contemplate the seizure of the strategically placed Trinity College. Some units saw virtually no action whatever while others, like the fourteen Volunteers at Mount Street Bridge, took on an entire British army battalion. The ill-fated Sherwood Foresters suffered more than two hundred casualties when they were caught in cross-fire as they marched from Dun Laoghaire towards the city centre.

The Easter Rising was, of course, doomed from the outset, but as we know, that wasn't the point. A military failure was turned into a political triumph when the British opted for a military rather than political response. No sensible politician would have approved the attenuated executions of the leaders of the rebellion. Pearse had achieved his blood sacrifice.

The Easter Rising began, ninety-nine years ago, on this day.

Broadcast 24 April 2015

10 April 1918
The British Parliament Proposes Conscription in Ireland

In late 1917 the British satirical magazine *Punch*, the *Charlie Hebdo* of its day, printed a cartoon, the context for which was the progress – or lack thereof – of the First World War. It depicted two men with a large comb divided into four equal parts marked 'England, Ireland, Scotland and Wales'. The Irish section was toothless. The magazine, not noted for its admiration of 'John Bull's other island', suggested that Ireland was not sending enough of its young men to stop machine-gun bullets on the Western Front and that it was high time the government did something about it. Compulsory military service for men between eighteen and forty years of age had been introduced in Britain in early 1916.

A few months after *Punch's* barb, Lloyd George's administration, which had hesitated to bring conscription to Ireland, finally grasped the nettle with the introduction in the House of Commons of an amendment to the Military Service Act. This raised the upper age limit in Britain to fifty and ended Ireland's exemption. The move came as a panic measure in the wake of the crippling and humiliating German offensive of 21 March 1918.

The Home Secretary, Sir George Cave, in proposing the extension of compulsory military service to Ireland, observed that 'We are advised that it will yield a large number of men'. The doubly bereaved Irish MP and British army officer, Captain William Archer Redmond, who had lost his father and uncle in the preceding nine months, inquired 'May I ask the right hon.

gentleman who advised him?' The implication was clear. The Irish, who had *volunteered* in respectable if unspectacular numbers, were not going to be *forced* to join the British army.

Cave was then interrupted by a passionate interjection from the Irish Party MP for Kerry North, Michael Flavin, who ominously shouted 'You come over and try it' at the government benches.

John Dillon, leader of the Irish Party since the death of John Redmond the previous month, pointed out that the raising of the military age and the extension of conscription to this country would have no impact in terms of manpower on the military disaster that was the German Spring offensive. It would take months to train the new conscripts, by which time it looked, at that point in the war, as if the Germans would be drinking champagne on the Champs-Elysées and accepting the surrender of France and Britain. As it happens, by the time the debate began, the German offensive had already begun to peter out, and it would not be long before the Allies rolled back the German gains and made the huge advances of their own that ended the war in November 1918.

That they did so without any Irish conscripts was a function of a concerted and determined campaign in Ireland. With a national strike, the opposition of the Roman Catholic hierarchy, a series of massive public meetings and the temporary shelving of political differences between the Irish Parliamentary Party and Sinn Féin, the British government concluded that it would cost more troops to enforce conscription than would be raised.

Had they not done so, and in the unlikely event that they had been successful in forcing Irishmen into the army, the death toll of Irish soldiers might well have greatly exceeded the 35,000 who did perish in the ironically titled 'war to end all wars'.

The proposal to extend compulsory military service to Ireland was brought to the floor of the House of Commons, ninety-seven years ago, on this day.

Broadcast 10 April 2015

17 April 1920
The Inquest into the Killing of the Lord Mayor of Cork, Tomás MacCurtain

There is a street in Cork named after him, and his was the first of two consecutive fatalities among Lord Mayors of Cork. The murder of Tomás MacCurtain on 20 March 1920 was followed seven months later by the death of his successor, Terence MacSwiney, after a hunger strike in Brixton prison.

MacCurtain was born on 20 March 1884, and was, therefore, shot dead on his thirty-sixth birthday. Of more consequence was that the assassination took place in front of his wife and one of his sons. His background was similar to that of many other republican figures of the early twentieth century. He was a member of the Gaelic League and a founding member of the Irish Volunteers, siding with the anti-war element when the organisation split in 1914.

MacCurtain would have been 'out' in 1916 but for the failure of his force of one thousand Cork Volunteers to receive orders to that effect from the Dublin rebels. After the Easter Rising he received his further education in revolutionary nationalism in Frongoch prison in North Wales. After his release in 1917 he took up the position of brigadier in the Cork IRA and was unsuccessful in an attempt in the early months of the Anglo-Irish war to assassinate Sir John French, the British Lord Lieutenant. In January 1920 he was elected to Cork City Council and was later elected Lord Mayor by his Sinn Féin party colleagues.

MacCurtain lived with his family in the Blackpool area of Cork. On 20 March 1920 a number of men with blackened faces – up to eight in all – ransacked his home and shot MacCurtain dead. It was one of a number of reprisal killings to take place on both sides. It has been suggested that McCurtain's killing was in retaliation for the murder, earlier that day, of Police Constable Murtagh on Pope's Quay. Whether organised retaliation would have occurred that quickly, within two hours of Murtagh's killing, is a moot point.

But who actually shot the Lord Mayor of Cork? The jury at his inquest had no doubt. The coroner, James J. McCabe, examined ninety-seven witnesses in all, sixty-four being members of the RIC. The inquest took nearly a month. The jury, unimpressed by conflicts of evidence among senior RIC officers in the city, issued a verdict of 'wilful murder' against British Prime Minister Lloyd George and against a number of policemen, some named, but with the actual killers described as 'unknown members of the RIC'.

More extra-judicial killings followed. Michael Collins made it his business to take revenge on any of the RIC officers alleged to have been involved in the assassination. The most prominent of these, RIC District Inspector Oswald Swanzy, the man accused of having ordered the attack, was himself murdered while leaving a church in Lisburn in August 1920. In a highly symbolic act, MacCurtain's revolver was used to shoot Swanzy dead. The killing, however, sparked retaliatory action against the Catholic residents of the town.

The jury in the inquest into the assassination of Tomás MacCurtain, Lord Mayor of Cork, delivered its telling verdict, ninety-five years ago, on this day.

Broadcast 17 April 2015

May

Playtime at the Kennedy compound

8 May 1597
The Death of Rebel Gaelic Chieftain
Fiach McHugh O'Byrne

Curse and swear Lord Kildare,
Fiach will do what Fiach will dare,
Now Fitzwilliam have a care,
Fallen is your star low.
Up with halbert, out with sword,
On we go for, by the Lord
Fiach McHugh has given the word 'Follow me up to Carlow'

So goes 'Follow Me up to Carlow', a song about Wicklow chieftain
Fiach McHugh O'Byrne, and one of the best-known songs in the
Irish traditional canon, although it was written many years after
the events that the chorus describes.

To suggest that Fiach McHugh O'Byrne was a thorn in the
side of the Tudor dynasty in Ireland would be to exaggerate hugely
the impact of a thorn. O'Byrne was nuisance and nemesis rolled
together.

He was born in 1534 and became chieftain of the O'Byrne clan
in his mid-forties. One of the main reasons why he was so despised
by British administrators in Ireland was because of his geographical
proximity to the Pale. Whenever O'Byrne chose to bite off another
piece of Tudor Dublin he didn't have far to go. And he chose to do
so on a regular basis.

Retaliating against him was not quite as straightforward. There was no M11 or GPS in the 1500s, so the Tudor armies sent against him had to make do with whatever tracks they could find and wasted many frustrating days searching in vain for Fiach.

When Red Hugh O'Donnell and Art O'Neill made their celebrated escape from Dublin Castle in 1592, it was to Glenmalure, O'Byrne's main redoubt, that they headed. Art O'Neill didn't make it, but a frostbitten Hugh O'Donnell did. O'Byrne sheltered him and sent him back to his own people in Donegal, from where too he made quite a nuisance of himself, along with Hugh O'Neill, in the Nine Years' War.

O'Byrne also made himself useful with the Earls of Kildare, who often had an ambiguous relationship with the English Crown. Fiach once peremptorily hanged an important witness to a threatening government investigation into the affairs of Gerald Fitzgerald, eleventh Earl of Kildare. Bumping off hostile witnesses didn't start with the Mafia.

During the Desmond Rebellion in 1580, the Lord Lieutenant, Lord Grey, led an army against the O'Byrnes. His plan was to attack Glenmalure. Like many a good plan brought to bear against Fiach, it failed miserably and Grey was forced to withdraw to Dublin with serious losses. The Battle of Glenmalure was O'Byrne's greatest triumph against the forces of Queen Elizabeth I.

Sadly, Fiach came to a bad end in 1597. He threw in his lot with O'Neill and O'Donnell in the Nine Years' War. In an engagement with English troops, assisted by some renegade members of his own clan, Fiach was captured and summarily beheaded with his own sword. His body was then cut up and the head and quarters were hung on pikes on the Dublin Castle walls. His head was then pickled and brought to London. It was a sad end for a redoubtable enemy of Tudor England.

Fiach McHugh O'Byrne, one of the last great Gaelic chieftains, died four hundred and eighteen years ago, on this day.

Broadcast 8 May 2015

9 May 1766
The Execution of the Hiberno-French Nobleman Thomas Lally

Thomas Arthur Lally was not quite as Irish as his name might suggest. He was born in France in 1702, son of Sir Gerald Lally from Tuam in Co. Galway, an Irish exile in France who had fought in the Jacobite Wars. The family was said to be able to trace its Irish ancestry back to Conn of the Hundred Battles. Like his father, Thomas Lally was destined for a military career. He joined the French army in 1721 and rose to command his own regiment in the Irish Brigade at the celebrated French victory against the British at Fontenoy in 1745. He was immediately promoted to Brigadier.

That same year he accompanied Prince Charles Edward Stuart, aka Bonnie Prince Charlie, to Scotland. But he shared in the Young Pretender's defeat and was forced to escape to France. While in Scotland he was given the titles of Earl of Moenmoyne, Viscount Ballymole and Baron Tollendally, by Prince Charles. Not surprisingly, given the Stuart defeat, none of the titles are to be found in *Burke's Peerage*.

When France's umpteenth war with Britain broke out in 1756 Lally was given command of a French expedition to India – France had Indian colonies of its own at the time. The objective was to get possession of those belonging to Britain – a project that initially met with some success. But things quickly began to go wrong for Lally's under-resourced force. He was beaten in a number of encounters with British forces – among them was a defeat by fellow Irishman Eyre Coote – and retreated to the city of Pondicherry. There he withstood a lengthy siege before conceding defeat in January 1761 and handing the city over to the British. Lally was sent as a prestigious prisoner to Britain. He must have wondered who would be scapegoated in France for the humiliation of this defeat. Would it be members of the French ministry or perhaps even the King himself, Louis XV?

He soon found out that he was to be the scapegoat. While in Britain, Lally discovered, to his chagrin, that he was being accused of treason in France. This was based on the surrender of Pondicherry. Instead of biding his time in England he sought permission from his captors to return to France on parole to defend his reputation. He was imprisoned in France for two years before he was tried, found guilty and beheaded in 1766. This was in the days prior to the French Revolution and the invention of the guillotine. The execution was carried out in front of a large crowd at the Place de l'Hotel de Ville in Paris. Lally was decapitated by sword. The infamous Marquis de Sade is said to have described the execution as botched, claiming that Lally had survived for more than a minute after the blow fell and had actually attempted to hold his head and neck together before he finally expired.

In his history of the French revolution, Thomas Carlyle describes Lally's execution as judicial murder. He describes how Lally was transported through the streets of Paris to his place of execution with a gag around his mouth to ensure that he was unable to protest at the injustice of the sentence against him. Two years after Lally's death he was posthumously pardoned by the new King, Louis XVI.

Thomas Arthur, Comte de Lally, was executed in Paris two hundred and forty-eight years ago, on this day.

Broadcast 9 May 2014

23 May 1798
The Rebellion of the United
Irishmen Begins in Dublin

It may come as a surprise to learn that the county of Wexford was once a Republic in its own right, as opposed to being merely part of one. I blame the French myself, as did the British administration in Ireland. Far too many people thought they could emulate the French revolution and get rid of tyrannical rule.

It all happened, of course, in May 1798, when the United Irishmen rose in rebellion in different parts of the country. The most successful and longest lasting of these disparate insurrections was in the Model County, but the rebellion itself kicked off in Dublin when small crowds of men set out from some of the poorer parts of the city, hoping to seize the symbolic Dublin Castle and other key public buildings.

So thoroughly infiltrated were the Dublin United Irishmen – one of their most inspirational leaders, Lord Edward Fitzgerald, had already been captured – that the rising stood little or no chance there. The militia sorted out the rebels and many simply abandoned their weapons and quietly slipped back to their homes. More successful were rebellions in the counties around Dublin, in Kildare, Meath and Wicklow – though opposition was mopped up quickly in those areas as well.

The most successful insurrection, other than that of the Northern United Irishmen in Co. Antrim, was in Wexford, an area not deemed worthy of that much attention by the Castle in its intelligence operations. That was a mistake. Despite losing its leader, Bagenal Harvey, before Wexford rose, the rebels retained leaders good enough to cause serious problems to the local militia. Harvey was captured after the authorities moved against him on the basis of information secured through the torture of leading United Irishman Anthony Perry. Perry had been pitch-capped by the North Cork Militia in Gorey. This delightful practice involved pouring hot tar onto the heads of rebels and tearing it off when it had cooled. Perry later got at least some of his own back when he was released, joined the rebels, and led a force at the Battle of Tuberneering on 4 June which destroyed much of the British force in North Wexford. A few days beforehand the citizens of Wexford had established their own republican regime.

The rebels had quickly taken Enniscorthy and then Wexford town itself, led by, among others, Perry, Fr. John Murphy and John Kelly – the 'Boy from Killane' in the folk song of that name – though he was highly unlikely to have been 'seven feet in height with some inches to spare'. For a fortnight the British army in Wexford was unable to inflict a serious defeat on the rebels, until the United Irishmen fell short of taking New Ross on 5 June. It was towards the end of the battle for New Ross that one of two infamous massacres of loyalist civilians took place at Scullabogue when two hundred men, women and children were herded into a farm building which was then burned, with the loss of all but two lives. The atrocity was probably in retaliation for the many outrages that had been committed by the largely Protestant Yeomanry forces in the weeks prior.

As the British General Gerard Lake, continued to make inroads on the rebels, defeating the bulk of their forces at Vinegar Hill on 21 June, a second massacre of loyalists took place on Wexford Bridge. Accordingly, it was there that Bagenal Harvey and John

Kelly were taken and hanged after the reverse at Vinegar Hill and the inevitable repercussions of that defeat. The British response to the rebellion was ferocious, all the more so as small bands of rebels continued to hold out in the county for some months. Many of those captured in 1798 were later brutally executed.

The United Irishmen's rebellion, which found its most successful expression in Co. Wexford, began in Dublin, two hundred and sixteen years ago, on this day.

Broadcast 23 May 2014

30 May 1807
The Duel of William Congreve Alcock and John Colclough

Irish elections can be boisterous and violent affairs, but none more so than the Co. Wexford election to the British House of Commons in 1807, just a few years after the Act of Union.

Among the contestants (who, unbeknownst to himself, included the playwright Richard Brinsley Sheridan) were two local grandees William Congreve Alcock and John Colclough. Colclough's brother, who gloried in the traditional Irish moniker of Caesar, had been the local MP but was a prisoner of war in France at the time the election was called. The Colcloughs, who were generally popular landlords, had lived at Tintern Abbey, a former monastery, since the sixteenth century.

The election campaign was a bitter one; polling was due to take place on 1 June, but with just two days to go, Alcock took exception to what he alleged was an attempt by Colclough to steal the support of tenants obligated to vote for him. In what appears like a piece of egregious over-reaction, he challenged Colclough to a duel and in the encounter that followed Alcock shot his political opponent dead. As the MP for Athlone, George Tierney, observed tartly, 'That's one way of getting an election'. As duelling was still socially acceptable in early nineteenth-century Ireland, Alcock was acquitted of murder and allowed to take his seat in the House of Commons. But he was not to continue in office for long – two years after the duel he was committed to an asylum. The Irish judge and memoirist, Jonah Barrington, wrote of Alcock that:

> *Alas! the acquitted duellist suffered more in mind than his victim had done in body. The horror of the scene, and the solemnity of the trial, combined to make a fatal inroad on his reason! He became melancholy; his understanding declined; a dark gloom enveloped his entire intellect; and an excellent young man and perfect gentleman at length sank into irrecoverable imbecility.*

But there is an interesting postscript to this sad tale. Not all those affected by the duel came out of it badly.

Colclough's estate at Tintern Abbey was managed by his steward, one James Kennedy. Because of the absence of Caesar Colclough in France, Kennedy continued to run the estate until Caesar's return in 1815. During that period something of the order of £80,000 disappeared. Nobody could pin it directly on the steward, but in 1818 Kennedy was dismissed at the behest of Caesar Colclough's wife, Jane Stratford Kirwan. The money remains unaccounted for. There are, however, persistent rumours that at least some of it may have been used a generation later to fund the migration to the USA of the Kennedy family in the 1840s, and perhaps even to set up the Boston saloon that became the basis of the family fortune. A descendant of James Kennedy, by the name of John Fitzgerald Kennedy, went on to become President of the United States of America in 1961.

Was the Kennedy fortune based on the tragic outcome of a tragic confrontation between two Irish aristocrats? Perish the thought.

William Congreve Alcock shot his opponent John Colclough dead in a duel, two hundred and seven years ago, on this day.

Broadcast 30 May 2014

15 May 1808
The Birth of Composer
Michael Balfe

Thirty-eight operas and two hundred and fifty songs is not an insignificant output for a forty-year career as a composer. Rossini? Verdi? Wagner?

None of the above; Balfe actually. Michael Balfe was born in Dublin in 1808 – though also associated with Wexford – and was the composer of the best-known nineteenth century opera to have come out of this country, *The Bohemian Girl*.

Early in his life he looked set to become a violin virtuoso rather than a composer. He was performing at the age of nine and playing in the Theatre Royal, Drury Lane, as a teenager. At one point in his life he even tried his luck as an opera singer, but he appears to have been better at writing arias than singing them. During his brief career as a singer, he did become a protégée of the great Rossini and once took the part of Figaro in a production of the *Barber of Seville* in Paris.

He spent most of his twenties in Italy where he began composing in earnest, mostly operas in Italian. When he left Italy for London in 1835 his career as a composer began to take off. Among his early successes was a piece called *Falstaff*, derived from Shakespeare's comedy, the *Merry Wives of Windsor* rather than the History plays.

The *Bohemian Girl*, loosely based on a story by Cervantes, was written when he was thirty-five and premiered at the Theatre Royal,

Drury Lane. It ran there for more than one hundred performances, and productions soon followed in New York, Dublin, Philadelphia, Vienna, Sydney, and throughout Europe and elsewhere. The opera was also quickly translated into Italian, German and French. The best-known song from the opera, still popular today, was 'I Dreamt I Dwelt in Marble Halls', in which the heroine recalls vague memories of a privileged childhood. Versions of the song have been recorded by singers as disparate as Dame Joan Sutherland and Enya. The opera remained a familiar part of the operatic repertoire until the 1930s and is still occasionally performed. A silent movie version, rather strange for an opera, was made in 1922. Laurel and Hardy produced a comic version in a 1936 film. James Joyce refers to the opera in two stories in his *Dubliners* collection and again in *Finnegans Wake*.

In later life Balfe became a musical director and conductor in London, working with, amongst others, the great Swedish soprano Jenny Lind. He continued to compose throughout his life and among his other notable successes was a setting of Tennyson's poem, 'Come into the Garden Maud'.

Balfe died in his rented country estate in Hertfordshire in 1870. He is buried in Kensal Green cemetery in London. Next door is the grave of his fellow Irish composer, William Vincent Wallace from Waterford.

Michael Balfe, best remembered today as the man who wrote *The Bohemian Girl*, was born two hundred and seven years ago, on this day.

Broadcast 15 May 2015

1 May 1837
The Birth of Mary Harris,
a.k.a. 'Mother Jones'

When your entire family, comprising a husband and four children, die from yellow fever, and then your business is destroyed in the Great Chicago fire, you might be tempted to just give up. But not Mary Harris Jones, who instead went from extreme adversity to become 'Mother Jones' – 'the most dangerous woman in America'. That, at least, was how American mine-owners saw her. She did give them good cause for their animosity.

Mary Harris was born in Cork city in 1837 and emigrated to Canada with her family as a teenager. As a qualified teacher, she moved to the USA and married George Jones, a union organiser, in Memphis, Tennessee. There she abandoned teaching and became a dressmaker.

It was in Memphis that she lost her family to disease. All her children were under five years of age. After that unthinkable tragedy she moved to Chicago and established a dressmaking business there. In 1871, the Great Chicago fire that killed three hundred people and destroyed nine square kilometres of the city took her business and house with it.

After losing everything, she threw in her lot with organised labour and some of the most iconic unions in American history, such as the United Mine Workers, the Knights of Labour and the Industrial Workers of the World, the latter better known as the 'Wobblies'. Given her personal trauma, her motto, 'pray for the dead and fight like hell for the living' is particularly poignant. She travelled the USA organising and motivating workers and their families to take action to improve their lot.

She was ardently opposed to the use of child labour. In 1903 she organised for children to march in their thousands from Philadelphia to the New York home of President Theodore Roosevelt, bearing banners with the slogan 'We want to go to school and not the mines'.

During a West Virginia miners' strike she ignored a court order secured by the mine-owners and in her subsequent trial the District Attorney, appropriately named Blizzard, declaimed that 'There sits the most dangerous woman in America ... She comes into a state where peace and prosperity reign ... crooks her finger [and] twenty thousand contented men lay down their tools and walk out'.

You might well have expected a female radical like Mother Jones to be a suffragist, but she wasn't. She was opposed to votes for women and female participation in politics. Her philosophy was, 'You don't need the vote to raise hell!' She was of the opinion that men should earn sufficient money to allow their wives to bring up their children. Equally unusually, she claimed to be considerably older than she actually was, possibly in the interests of self-protection, hence the nickname 'Mother' Jones.

She became so influential that, in the case of a mining strike in Colorado, she was able to force the infamous 'robber baron' John D. Rockefeller into a face-to-face meeting and extract significant concessions from him on behalf of the miners.

Denounced in the Senate as the 'grandmother of all agitators', she responded by saying 'I hope to live long enough to become the great-grandmother of all agitators'. This she did, dying at the age of ninety-three.

Mary Harris, a.k.a. 'Mother Jones', labour activist and champion of the working man, was born one hundred and seventy-eight years ago on what, appropriately, has become International Labour Day.

Broadcast 1 May 2015

22 May 1849
The Death of Novelist
Maria Edgeworth

She didn't have a lot of time for Jane Austen, and she earned more money from her books than did the Queen of Irony during her lifetime. She was a frequent correspondent of Sir Walter Scott, another celebrated contemporary. She was also hugely important in the development of the novel and of children's writing. Not bad for a woman who spent much of her life in rural Longford.

Maria Edgeworth, although seen as an Irish novelist, was actually born in England, the second of twenty-two children of Richard Lovell Edgeworth, who was married four times. She moved to Ireland with her father at the age of five, after the death of her mother. She spent much of her teenage years looking after her younger siblings and was, essentially, educated by her father, whom she also assisted in managing the family estate at Edgeworthstown. Her father was a huge influence, some would say far too great an influence, on her writing. She claimed to have written only to please him.

Edgeworth took up what would today be identified as liberal causes in her novels. She championed the underprivileged of her adopted country and sought to counteract English literary stereotypes of Ireland in her work. In addition she parodied elements of her own landed class, especially in her most famous novel, the often hilarious *Castle Rackrent* – written without her father's knowledge – where the worst excesses of landlordism are satirised. In much of Edgeworth's *oeuvre* the peasantry are dignified and the aristocracy rapacious. In *Letters for Literary Ladies* she pleaded the case for the proper education of women. Later, in the novel *Helen,* written after her father's death and not set in Ireland, she introduced a female politician to English literature.

Castle Rackrent, her first novel, published in 1800, was an instant success. Narrated by an employee of the Rackrents, Thady Quirk, it predicts the rise of the Catholic middle class. The novel, actually not much more than a novella, brought her to the attention of Sir Walter Scott. The two writers became friends and visited each other in Ireland and Scotland.

Such was the nature of her writing that in 1798, after the defeat of the French invasion in the west of Ireland, the windows of Edgeworth House were stoned because the family was suspected of having radical sympathies. In fact Edgeworth was a supporter of the Union, but also an advocate of Catholic Emancipation.

While Jane Austen was a great fan of Edgeworth, the admiration was not entirely mutual. Austen sent Edgeworth a presentation copy of *Emma* in 1816. Edgeworth was not impressed with a novel that now ranks behind only *Pride and Prejudice* as Austen's greatest achievement. The gift went unacknowledged and Edgeworth wrote to a friend about *Emma* that 'It has no story'.

She wrote little from the 1820s onwards, concentrating on the management of the family estate. Then, in 1845, when she was in her late seventies, the disaster of the Great Famine struck. Unlike many other landlords, who adopted a callous attitude to their starving tenants, Edgeworth was one of those who worked selflessly for her tenants. With her own money she purchased food from the USA which was distributed amongst her tenantry and others. The

Edgeworth's estate barely avoided bankruptcy and was purchased by carpetbaggers under the terms of the Encumbered Estates Act. Her compassion has, however, been somewhat exaggerated as her charity only extended as far as tenants who had paid their rent.

Maria Edgeworth, educationalist, farm manager, essayist and novelist, died one hundred and sixty-six years ago, on this day.

Broadcast 22 May 2015

2 May 1882
The 'Kilmainham Treaty' and the Release of Parnell from Jail

Charles Stewart Parnell was known as 'The Uncrowned King of Ireland' and Kings used to have the power to make treaties or at least send someone to conclude them in their place. But Parnell, in 1882, was partly responsible for the 'Treaty That Wasn't'. It became known as the Kilmainham Treaty, called after the impressive jail of that name rather than the salubrious suburb of Dublin 8.

At this time, there was chaos in the Irish countryside as the eviction of tenants escalated when agricultural depression hit what we would now call 'the developed world'. Ireland was, at the time, only included within the ambit of the developed world by default, as part of the United Kingdom. Evictions inevitably led to agrarian unrest – retaliation in the form of attacks on bailiffs, agents, and landlords, not to mention assaults on so-called 'land grabbers' who moved into the farms of families who had been evicted. Most of these attacks were carried out by Ribbonmen, members of agrarian secret societies. The murder rate soared and the Royal Irish Constabulary found itself under huge pressure to make arrests and secure convictions in a rural environment where Catholic and nationalist juries were ill-disposed to convict even the most obviously guilty Ribbonmen.

115

The British government response was, as always, to take a benign, far-sighted softly-softly approach.

That's actually completely untrue. They did what they normally did and imposed the sort of coercive measures that would never have been tolerated in England, Scotland or Wales. In fairness, however, they would probably have been unnecessary outside of stroppy old Ireland.

In essence, *Habeas Corpus* was suspended – the government dispensed with the need to bring anyone to trial and produce actual evidence of wrongdoing in order to convict them. It was sufficient merely to suspect that they had been up to no good in order to throw them in jail. One of the first victims was Parnell himself, arrested in Dublin by the famed Metropolitan policeman Superintendent John Mallon, and detained at the pleasure of Her Majesty in Kilmainham Jail.

Parnell resided there for six months, experiencing no difficulty whatever in keeping up a passionate correspondence with his partner Katharine O'Shea. Ultimately it was her ambitious husband who 'sprang' the Uncrowned King. William O'Shea, always a man with an eye to the main chance, brokered a deal whereby Parnell promised to do his best to rein in the agrarian extremists who were making things unpleasant for the poor landlords, while William Gladstone's government agreed to introduce remedial legislation to improve the lot of impoverished tenant farmers. The alternative was a continuation of the anarchy that reigned while the entire Irish political leadership was in stir.

As an added extra, Parnell tossed in a tasty morsel for the Liberal government in the shape of a potential future political alliance. This was what riled many of Parnell's supporters and led to both sides denying that the agreement ever existed. Gallons of cold water were poured over allegations that a deal had been done by both Parnell and Gladstone, but O'Shea's preening and the exponential increase in his normal level of smugness told insiders that some sort of compact had been arrived at to allow for the release of Parnell from jail. It was all a monumental waste of time as four days after Parnell got out of Kilmainham, the shadowy subversive organisation, the Invincibles, murdered Gladstone's nephew Lord Frederick Cavendish – the new Chief Secretary – and his second in command Thomas H. Burke in Phoenix Park. And it was back to the messy status quo for another few years.

Charles Stewart Parnell was released from Kilmainham Jail on the basis of what might be described today as 'certain agreed modalities' but definitely not a treaty of any kind, one hundred and thirty-two years ago, on this day.

Broadcast 2 May 2014

16 May 1907
The Birth of Olympic Hurdler Bob Tisdall

It was Monday 1 August 1932. In one glorious hour at the Olympic Stadium in Los Angeles, Ireland won two track and field gold medals. The second gold was won by hammer thrower Pat O'Callaghan, a surprise champion in 1928 when, as a relative novice, he had only been included on the Irish team to gain experience of top class competition. There was no surprise at all at his follow-up victory four years later.

The first of the two medals that day, however, was won by a tall, handsome four hundred metres hurdler, Robert Morton Tisdall. Born in Ceylon (now Sri Lanka), Tisdall was brought up in Nenagh, Co. Tipperary – home to two previous Irish Olympic gold medallists Johnny Hayes and Matt McGrath, who had competed for the USA in the early 1900s at a time when there was, of course, no Irish Olympic team.

Tisdall had the right pedigree. His father had been an Irish sprint champion and his mother had played hockey for Ireland. The twenty-five-year-old Tisdall had given up a fabulous job just to compete in Los Angeles. He had landed on his feet during the Great Depression by becoming an aide to a wealthy young Indian Maharajah on an extensive European tour. That plum job went by the board in the fulfilment of the dream of Olympic success.

Tisdall had already shown athletic promise at the University of Cambridge where he managed to win four events in the annual encounter with Oxford – he finished first not only in the two hurdle races but in the long jump and, bizarrely, the shot putt. In the lead up to the Los Angeles Games, Tisdall was, essentially, a low hurdles runner over two hundred and twenty yards. But in 1932, never having actually run in the event, he wrote to the President of the Olympic Council of Ireland, Eoin O'Duffy – taking time off from his duties as Ireland's leading fascist – and asked to be considered for selection for the four hundred metres hurdles. Tisdall qualified to compete in the event by winning the national four hundred and forty yards hurdles event in Croke Park in 1932.

His training in California was not ideal. There were no hurdles available at the team training camp so he collected driftwood and improvised hurdles on a greyhound track. This took quite some time – just as he got ready for his first run someone switched on the mechanical rabbit. One by one the electronic bunny smashed his driftwood hurdles. Tisdall eventually found a track with hurdles at a local girls' school where he was allowed to train.

He won his heat with considerable ease. A recording of his semi-final victory can be seen on YouTube. It's quite amazing how easily he won this race, almost jogging to the line after the last hurdle, running from the outside lane. Astonishingly, after virtually pulling up and walking home almost nonchalantly, he still equalled the Olympic record. It was Tisdall's fifth ever run in the event.

In the final he faced three Olympic gold medallists: Glenn Hardin and Morgan Taylor of the USA, and David Cecil, Lord Burghley of Great Britain. He creamed the lot of them, setting a new world best time in the process and becoming the first four hundred metres hurdler to break fifty-two seconds. Ironically, however, it was the silver medallist, Glenn Hardin, who was credited with a new world record of 51.85 – Tisdall had knocked over the final hurdle and under the rules, changed not long afterwards, he was denied the record.

Tisdall took consolation in his magnificent gold medal and in the fact that at a subsequent gala dinner in Los Angeles he found himself seated between the celebrated aviator Amelia Earhart and the Hollywood movie star Douglas Fairbanks Jr.

Tisdall, who brought honour and pride to a newly-created state, barely a decade in existence at the time, lived to be ninety-seven years of age. He ran in the Sydney Olympics torch relay at the age of ninety-four.

Robert Morton Tisdall, Irish Olympic gold medallist, was born one hundred and seven years ago, on this day.

Broadcast 16 May 2014

29 May 1917
The Birth of US President
John F. Kennedy

It's one of the most popular 'what ifs' of the last fifty years; 'What if it had been raining on 22 November 1963 in Dallas?'

Obviously there would have been no Presidential open-top motorcade, and Lee Harvey Oswald, or the Mafia, or the man on the grassy knoll, or the four French hired assassins from Marseilles, or whatever other conspiracy theory you subscribe to, would have been denied the opportunity to demonstrate his or their peerless marksmanship and John Fitzgerald Kennedy, thirty-fifth President of the United States of America, would probably have seen out his first term and been re-elected in November 1964.

Of course there's another great 'what if' when it comes to the career of John F. Kennedy. What if his older brother, Joseph Kennedy Jr, had survived World War Two? Would John F. ever have become President? His domineering father, Joseph Sr had always intended that Joe Jr. would occupy the White House.

John F. Kennedy was, arguably, the first conscious political 'brand'. With iconographers like Theodore Sorenson and Pierre Salinger cultivating and honing the Kennedy narrative, he could hardly fail. Fifty years later he is a mythic figure. Myth = branding + time.

The skein of myth, however, is easily unravelled. For example, he wasn't even the youngest American president. When Theodore Roosevelt took over the office after the assassination of William McKinley in 1901, he was nine months younger than Kennedy.

JFK's credentials as a supposed political progressive don't stand up to much examination either. In 1957 he opposed Eisenhower's civil rights legislation. He persisted, when in office, with the Democratic Party practice of appointing dodgy judges to federal courts in the south. One such JFK appointee, a man called Harold Cox, once described African-Americans as 'chimpanzees' *after* he had been elevated to the federal bench.

During his first term as a senator Kennedy teamed up with the darling of the Republican right, Barry Goldwater, to try and keep rock and roll music off American radio stations. He connived in the assassination of a supposed ally (and fellow Roman Catholic), Ngo Dinh Diem, the beleaguered president of South Vietnam.

But he also achieved a lot of good during a very short life. Take just one month of his Presidency, for example – June 1963. On 10 June this apparent Cold War warrior made a major foreign policy speech at the American University in Washington DC. In a world dominated by ideas of mutually assured destruction he appeared to extend an olive branch to the Russians.

The following day, after Governor George Wallace of Alabama was forced by Federal intervention to, quite literally, step aside and allow two African American students pass into the campus of the University of Alabama, Kennedy made a largely improvised address on national radio and TV, promising equal access to public schools and enhanced voting rights to African-American citizens.

Then, on 26 June he made his famous 'Ich bin ein Berliner' speech (the 'ein' was superfluous) a short time after viewing the newly erected Berlin wall. He also, of course, dropped into Ireland for four days on his way home.

Not a bad month's work really.

John Fitzgerald Kennedy, thirty-fifth President of the USA, was born ninety-eight years ago, on this day.

Broadcast 29 May 2015

June

Overthrown by a woman's gaze

20 June 1210
King John of England Lands at Waterford

King John has had a pretty bad rap from history. While he did deserve it to some extent, he was hardly worthy of the intense vilification of future generations. In popular mythology he is the villain-in-chief of the Robin Hood legends, in cahoots with the Sheriff of Nottingham to rob simple peasants of their livelihoods. He is the evil younger brother of the valiant Richard the Lionheart, who spent most of his reign in the service of Christianity retaking the shrines of the Holy Land from Muslim invaders. In the movie about his rather interesting family, *The Lion in Winter,* he was one of the sons of Eleanor of Aquitaine and King Henry II, he tends to snivel and skulk quite a lot.

That's the mythology. The reality is quite different. For a start there probably was no Robin Hood and even if there was, he was just as likely to have lived up to his surname as he was to have robbed from the rich and given to the poor. As for Richard the Lionheart, he spent most of his reign as King of England ignoring his subjects while pursuing his hobby of killing Muslims in the Crusades. He got the money for waging war by selling public offices to the highest bidder. Eventually he cost his subjects a shed-load of money when he got himself captured by Duke Leopold of Austria and was ransomed by the German Emperor Henry VI.

King John's bad reputation was gained when he spent much of Richard's ten-year reign plotting against his big brother. But then what's a guy supposed to do? They weren't particularly fraternal to begin with, and then Richard made matters worse by abandoning the family store and leaving it wide open to shoplifters. Then there was the whole 'Lionheart' thing. Red rag to a royal bull, really.

Of course John was neither a popular nor a successful King. He managed to lose most of England's French dominions and in trying to get them back annoyed the barons. This led to Magna Carta being forced down his throat after a successful rebellion. The Great Charter, signed at Runnymede in 1215, was the first negotiated curb on kingly power in England.

Five years before he submitted to the barons he went after two of their number in Ireland. King John landed here with an army in 1210 in an attempt to put manners on the de Lacys – Walter, the Earl of Meath, and Hugh, Earl of Ulster. He landed at Crook in Co. Waterford, giving rise to some confusion about the origins of the phrase 'by hook or by crook'. One version has it that had John not landed at Crook he would have come ashore nearby at Hook Head – hence his invasion of Ireland would have taken place 'by hook or by crook'. There are, however, umpteen other versions of how the phrase originated. John's visit was fairly successful and the De Lacys ceased to be a major irritant for him as a result.

Six years later he died, after reneging on Magna Carta and going back to war with his barons. He claimed that he had signed it under duress. He is said to have died of dysentery, not the kind of thing you associate with the deaths of kings.

King John, the only English monarch of that name, landed in Ireland nine hundred and four years ago, on this day.

Broadcast 20 June 2014

12 June 1730
The Robbery of the Treasure Ship the *Golden Lion* in Kerry

The small, picturesque, coastal town of Ballyheigue in Co. Kerry is located close to Banna Strand, which briefly played host to Sir Roger Casement in Easter Week of 1916 before he was rounded up by the RIC and escorted to London to be hanged on 4 August. Another ill-fated tourist in the area, in 1731, was a Danish ship named the *Golden Lion*, en route from Copenhagen to India, which made an impromptu visit to an inconvenient sandbank and never left. It's by far the most interesting of some twenty-six shipwrecked vessels around the village.

What made the story of the *Golden Lion* so compelling was the fact that, in addition to its captain Johan Heitman and the eighty-six other Danish crew-members, it also carried twelve sizeable chests loaded with silver bullion.

Ker-ching indeed!

Although the ship was not entirely wrecked and might well have been floated off the rocks, the locals were having none of it. Their hospitality knew no bounds when they discovered what the cargo was composed of. The eighty-seven Danes were rapidly rescued and far more generously treated than their marauding ninth- and tenth-century predecessors would have been had they been spotted off the Kerry coast.

Not that the local grandee, Thomas Crosbie, was fooled by the willingness of the local population to share their meagre fare with their Viking guests. He smelled a rat and decided that the locals were up to no good. He raced, post haste, to the beach where the *Golden Lion* lay stranded and chased away anyone he felt might have designs upon the cargo. He then spirited away the bullion himself, just for safe keeping you understand. This was, of course, perfectly acceptable because he was an avaricious landlord and not a starving peasant. Contemporary records refer to the Good Samaritan Crosbie as having '[gone] to the strand, [driven] back possible villains, comforted the sailors and had the silver transported to his own home'.

The silver was held in a tower on Crosbie's premises until arrangements could be made to house it in a safer place. Undoubtedly, the altruistic aristocrat – if that isn't a contradiction in terms – had no intention of claiming any reward for his act of mercy. If he did have plans for the silver, they never came to fruition; he did not get an opportunity to stake any such claim owing to the fact that the silver was then stolen. Tragically, given the scale of his generosity and public-spiritedness, Crosbie died before he got a chance to restore the bullion to its rightful owners. Whatever Crosbie's intentions might have been, his widow was not at all philanthropic. She demanded salvage payments from the Danish owners. Choosing to ignore the role of Thomas Crosbie in saving their dosh from the depredations of the North Kerry peasantry, the Danes counter-claimed that the ship and its contents were not salvage as it had not been in danger of sinking – which was rather beside the point really. Possession is, after all, nine tenths of the law.

While the matter was being adjudicated, around one hundred enterprising locals decided to intervene. Ballyheigue also happens to have been the birthplace of the great Irish economist Richard Cantillon, who invented the word 'entrepreneur'. He might well have described this group in such terms. Most of the North Kerry entrepreneurial class, albeit with blackened faces, surrounded the Crosbie household, broke into the tower, killed two of the Danish guards and made off with the loot on carts. Cantillon wrote in the early eighteenth century about the movement of gold and silver through the economy. However, this was probably not the sort of movement he had in mind.

The theft was believed to have been carried out by certain members of the Kerry upper crust. Sir Maurice Crosbie of Ardfert, a relative of the late lamented Thomas, conducted an investigation. The Danish Asiatic Company offered a generous reward of ten per cent of the value of the cargo for its recovery. One of the alleged robbers turned informer and ten men were charged with the theft. All were acquitted at a subsequent trial in Dublin that was a bizarre saga in itself, involving perjury, suicide and the suspected poisoning of a witness.

To date, just over £7,000 worth of the bullion has been recovered. The rest may well have all been melted down by now or transported out of the area. However, far be it from me to spark a stampede of silver prospectors to the pristine Kerry coastline, but there has to be an outside chance that it might be buried somewhere near Ballyheigue. Think about that one for a moment.

The Revenue Commissioners announced that the *Golden Lion* had been relieved of its cargo, two hundred and eighty-five years ago, on this day.

Broadcast 12 June 2015

19 June 1841
The Birth of George Arthur French, Head 'Mountie'

The extended French family of Roscommon has, in its various branches, produced numerous individuals of note. Percy French, the composer and performer of comic songs such as 'The Mountains of Mourne' and 'Come back Paddy Reilly to Ballyjamesduff' is the best-known and best-loved. Sir John French, first Commander of the British Expeditionary Force in the First World War, and who later became Irish Lord Lieutenant, probably wouldn't be *quite* as popular in this jurisdiction.

Somewhere in between is George Arthur French, born in Roscommon in 1841. His principal claim to fame is that, for a period of almost three years in the 1870s, he was head 'mountie'.

After the Confederation of Canada was formed in 1867, the new federal institutions suddenly had a lot of responsibility for the vast expanse of North-West Canada. Up to that point the Hudson's Bay Company had ruled the roost there and maintained the peace between a few fur trappers and a lot of indigenous tribes.

The Canadian government – which heretofore had done little more than police the country's big cities – now had to set up a mobile police force to cover an area about the size of Western Europe and protect Canada's borders from the incursion of American 'ne'er do wells' and illegal whiskey traders. So they modelled their police force on the Royal Irish Constabulary, put an Irishman in charge, and, very wisely, given the distances involved, placed them all on horseback. The new force became known as the North West Mounted Police. In due course, 1920 to be precise, it would become the Royal Canadian Mounted Police, or 'the mounties' – who, allegedly, always got their man, (female criminality in nineteenth-century Canada being very rare).

Because the native tribes were accustomed to seeing British army uniforms, rather than confuse the issue, the mounties were dressed up in red tunics and blue breeches.

George Arthur French, a Sandhurst-trained British army Colonel, was given command as the first permanent Commissioner of the North West Mounted Police. He duly led the force, around three hundred strong, on a long march west to take up their duties in the foothills of the Rockies. Their first object was to clear the American whiskey traders, most of them from the US territory of Montana, out of Indian lands. These nineteenth-century bootleggers, among whom the most prominent was another Irishman, Johnny Healy, had been plaguing the Blackfeet tribe in particular. Hearing of the impending arrival of the Mounties, the whiskey peddlers retreated across the border and continued to ply their trade in the western USA.

French continued as Commissioner for a couple of years before falling foul of Canadian politics and resigning in 1876. He went on to do a similar job in India and Australia and also returned to the British army where he attained the rank of Major General. In the Australian state of Queensland he acquired a reputation as a strike-breaker, on one occasion ordering his militia troops to fix bayonets against a group of strikers.

On his return to England in 1902 he was supposed to retire, but instead he spent the next nineteen years guarding the Crown Jewels. Lest there be any confusion, I am, of course, referring to the ones owned by the British monarchy and housed in the Tower of London.

Major General George Arthur French KCMG, native of Roscommon, and the original head Mountie, was born one hundred and seventy-four years ago, on this day.

Broadcast on 19 June 2015

27 June 1846
The Irish Nationalist Politician Charles Stewart Parnell is Born

No one could have predicted that the hesitant, almost inarticulate candidate for the Irish Parliamentary Party in the by-election in Dublin in 1874 would go on to be proclaimed the 'Uncrowned King of Ireland' and then brought to earth by the same people who had deified him in the first place.

For most of the first thirty years of his life Charles Stewart Parnell was a member of the family who were the benevolent landlords of Avondale in Co. Wicklow – an estate of four thousand acres that produced a modest income by the standards of the late 19th century. Parnell did what most of the members of his class did. He rode to hounds in the winter and played cricket in the summer – he was a decent batsman and wicketkeeper.

Then, suddenly, at the age of twenty-eight, he offered himself to the Irish Parliamentary Party, then led by Isaac Butt, as a candidate for the vacant seat in County Dublin. As he could afford to pay for his own campaign and didn't have to worry about any loss of earnings should he win the seat – ordinary MPs were not paid until the early 20th century – he got the nod from the party bosses. They quickly regretted their decision. The young Charles Stewart Parnell was a dreadful candidate. He could hardly put two words together and was so nervous as a public speaker that he could do little more than stammer on the hustings. The electorate was unimpressed and he was easily defeated.

He was given a second chance and did better the following year, winning a by-election in Meath. For two years Parnell kept his own counsel in the House of Commons. He watched and waited. Then, in a move apparently out of character with his social status, he threw in his lot with a group of converted Fenians and blocked much House of Commons business by filibustering – making long speeches on very little indeed – much to the annoyance of British MPs and most of the Irish ones as well.

Parnell would go on to lead his party, deliver some significant land reform, and appreciably advance the cause of Home Rule before his involvement in the divorce of Katharine O'Shea brought him crashing to earth.

Parnell, though briefly beloved of the nationalist Irish, was not held in such high esteem by many of his party colleagues. He was seen as aloof, arrogant, and often lazy. Unlike, for example, other Victorian politicians, who were enthusiastic correspondents, Parnell would not have been good on email. He treated the reams of correspondence that arrived for him on a daily basis with utter contempt. He rarely opened a letter, leaving that to others to do on his behalf. He was very superstitious, with a particular aversion for the month of October. Naturally, that was the month, in 1891, in which he died at the age of 45. Bizarrely, for someone who led the Irish constitutional nationalist movement for a momentous decade, he also loathed and feared the colour green.

Charles Stewart Parnell, politician, 'Uncrowned King' and chromophobe, was born one hundred and sixty-eight years ago, on this day.

Broadcast 27 June 2014

13 June 1865
The Birth of Poet W. B. Yeats in Dublin

William Butler Yeats, Ireland's first Nobel Literature Laureate – he received the award in 1923, two years before George Bernard Shaw – was born in Sandymount in Dublin in 1865. However, he spent much of his early life in Co. Sligo, which he considered to be his spiritual home. Rather surprisingly, painting rather than poetry was more in the Yeats bloodline. His father and brother, both called John, were distinguished painters, as was his ancestor Jervis Yeats, a Williamite soldier who benefitted from the defeat of King James in 1690.

Despite his impressive corpus of poetry and the fact that people constantly quote some of his best lines – how many 'Terrible Beauties' have been born since he wrote 'Easter 1916'? – Yeats is probably best known, in popular consciousness at least, for his doomed relationship with Maud Gonne. They first met in 1889 and according to Yeats she brought into his life 'a sound, as of a Burmese gong'. Presumably that was intended as a compliment but it was hardly designed to set the pulses of the twenty-three-year-old beauty racing. He first proposed to her in 1891. She refused him. He waited for another eight years before trying again. With the same result. He popped the question for a third time in 1900. Again, her answer was 'no'. Proving that he was a perennial optimist, or someone who just didn't take 'no' for an answer, he tried again in 1901. He got 'no' for an answer.

A few years later she horrified Yeats by marrying fellow Irish nationalist John McBride and, to his additional chagrin, became a Roman Catholic into the bargain. The marriage, to Yeats's intense satisfaction, was a disaster.

In 1908 Yeats had the even greater satisfaction of finally, after almost twenty years of forbearance, consummating his relationship with Maud Gonne. How well it went from her point of view can possibly be surmised from the letter she sent him in January 1909 suggesting that artists who abstained from sex would reap the rewards in their work. Either way, they never re-consummated their relationship.

Yeats was very much a public figure throughout the early part of the twentieth century. His co-founding of the Abbey Theatre, his aristocratic nationalism – which apparently included membership of the revolutionary organisation the Irish Republican Brotherhood – and two stints as a Senator of the newly-formed Irish Free State, ensured that he did not live the stereotypical life of the secluded, reclusive poet.

After the execution of Major John McBride in 1916, he proposed to Maud Gonne for a fifth time. Again he was rejected. He then turned his attention to her daughter Iseult, with the same result. Eventually Yeats did find happiness in his marriage to Georgie Hyde-Lees, who, although only half the poet's age, became his accomplice in some strange spiritualistic experiments and was an excellent partner for the ageing artist.

W. B. Yeats, a man whose tangled love-life inspired wonderful poetry, was born one hundred and forty-nine years ago, on this day.

Broadcast 13 June 2014

5 June 1916
The Death of Lord Kitchener,
Secretary of State for War

A number of highly significant Irishmen died violently in 1916: Patrick Pearse, Tom Clarke, James Connolly, to name but a few, who were shot in May. Pacifist Francis Sheehy Skeffington had also been summarily executed during the Easter Rising. His brother-in-law, Tom Kettle, barrister, poet and former MP, followed them all in September when he died at the Battle of Ginchy on the Western Front.

In between, another famous Irishman came to an unfortunate end. However, not many people realise that Herbert, Lord Kitchener, hero of Omdurman, scourge of the Boers and Secretary of State for War in the British Cabinet, was actually Irish. It was not something he tended to highlight himself.

But he was, in fact, as much a Kerryman as Mick O'Dwyer or John B. Keane. He was born Horatio Herbert Kitchener on 24 June 1850 in Ballylongford, near Listowel. His father, Lieutenant Colonel Henry Horatio Kitchener, had purchased land under the terms of the Encumbered Estates Act designed to buy out bankrupt property owners after the Famine – so a sort of nineteenth-century NAMA.

Kitchener left Kerry at the age of fourteen when the family moved to Switzerland for the health of his ailing mother. The future war-lord appears to have nurtured a similar attitude to his native land as that other great nineteenth-century military figure, the Duke of Wellington. Like a lot of other Anglo-Irish grandees with a minimal knowledge of their country of birth, Kitchener's dislike of the Irish did not stop him from claiming to have an informed insight into how the country should be governed. Kitchener was for lots of stick and very little carrot.

Not that his counsel on the subject would have been widely canvassed. Kitchener made his reputation in faraway wars, starting with the Sudan and his victory at the Battle of Omdurman in 1898. There he showed his compassionate side by digging up the remains of the Mahdi, slayer of General Gordon in the humiliating Battle of Khartoum in the 1880s, and having his bones scattered. Even Winston Churchill, not renowned for his squeamishness, who was covering the war as a reporter, was disgusted with the levels of slaughter, particularly of Sudanese prisoners.

The *de facto* Kerryman also made his presence felt in the Boer War where his scorched earth policy and his creation of concentration camps brought the Boers to their knees in the most ruthless possible fashion. Kitchener didn't have much time for uppity colonials.

When World War One broke out Kitchener was quickly appointed Secretary of State for War and his iconic moustache and index finger were used as recruiting devices on the famous 'Your Country Needs You' posters.

In a final gesture of solidarity with his native land, Kitchener refused all requests for the incorporation of the southern Irish Volunteers as a unit into his New Army, despite the passage of the Home Rule Act before hostilities commenced. The Ulster Volunteers, however, signatories of a covenant pledging opposition to a democratic decision taken by the British parliament, became the 36th Ulster Division. Consistency to Kitchener was as dangerous a vice as sentimentality.

Kitchener, despite his pathological hatred of journalists, probably owed his appointment to the Cabinet in 1914 to a newspaper campaign designed to force the Liberal government to put this crusty old Tory in charge of the army and Navy. Having 'created' him, the newspapers of the Dublin-born Press Baron Lord Northcliffe sought to undo their own handiwork when they campaigned against him in 1915. They blamed the Secretary of State for War for a chronic shortage of shells on the Western Front. The public sided with the most famous moustache in history and burned copies of the *Times* and the *Mail* in the streets.

In June 1916 Kitchener set sail for talks in Russia on board the HMS *Hampshire*. The ship hit a German mine and sank, taking the Secretary of State for War with it. The reluctant Kerryman died, ninety-nine years ago, on this day.

Broadcast 5 June 2015

6 June 1944
Irishmen Fight in Operation
Overlord, 'D-Day'

It was the biggest seaborne invasion in military history. Meticulous preparations for Operation Overlord, the allied invasion of Europe in June 1944, began three years beforehand. Knowledge was confined to an elite group and never seeped outside of that close circle.

Thousands of Irishmen, many from the neutral Irish Free State, were involved in what would become known as 'D-Day'. The Royal Ulster Rifles was the only regiment with two battalions in operation on the day of the invasion of Normandy. The 1st battalion went in on board gliders and landed behind enemy lines; the 2nd battalion took the more traditional route.

One Irishman centrally involved was the future Lord Killanin. He was a staff officer in an armoured division. Despite being completely 'in the know' about the invasion plans, he was allowed back to Ireland on leave a fortnight before 'D-Day'. A few sherries too many in the wrong place and the entire plan might have been betrayed unknowingly.

The Sweeney family, who ran the meteorological station and lighthouse at Blacksod Bay in Co. Mayo played their own small but significant part in proceedings. The invasion had originally been planned for 5 June, but the weather was so vile that it was temporarily abandoned. If it could not happen on 6 or 7 June it would have to be postponed for a number of weeks, so that the moon and the tides aligned to maximum benefit. The weather needed to break sufficiently to allow for the invasion to take place. When Edward Sweeney at Blacksod lighthouse in Mayo confirmed that there was a brief window of suitable weather, Eisenhower ordered the operation to proceed. The temporary improvement in the weather took the Germans completely by surprise.

The commanders of the invading force expected a renewal of chemical warfare on a scale not seen since the First World War. Paddy Devlin from Galway, waiting on board a glider with the rest of the 1st Royal Ulster Rifles, remembers being 'issued with new suits of battle dress that were as stiff as planks and had a white residue on them.' They were told that they had been soaked in a solution to prevent lice. In fact, the uniforms were designed to counteract gas – Devlin chose to believe the story about the lice.

The greatest loss of life was suffered at one of the American beaches, code-named Omaha – the tragedy is graphically depicted in the opening scene of *Saving Private Ryan*. Dubliner David McCaughey operated a landing craft at Omaha. His vessel was hit early on in the landings and he was forced to sit out most of the day on the foreshore, sheltering in his stricken craft. He became conscious of two oddities. The first was the figure '1' in red on the backs of the helmets of the dead US soldiers who had pitched forward when struck by bullets or shrapnel. This was the insignia of the 1st Infantry Division, nicknamed, 'The Big Red One'.

The second memorable feature of the day was an odd transparent material blowing across the beach in huge quantities. McCaughey remembered seeing this wrapped around the soldiers' guns. They had removed it when they reached the beach. He found out later that he was looking at polythene for the first time. It is a sad fact of life that war tends to spark scientific innovation.

Operation Overlord, the allied invasion of German-occupied France, took place seventy years ago, on this day.

Broadcast 6 June 2014

26 June 1963
US President John F. Kennedy Begins his Official State Visit to Ireland

John Fitzgerald Kennedy was elected with just over forty-nine per cent of the votes cast in the 1960 race for the White House. While in office, his approval rating rarely dipped below sixty per cent. After the Cuban Missile Crisis his ratings were in the high 70s. In a poll of 1,960 voters taken after his death, seventy per cent claimed to have cast their ballots for him as President.

But in Ireland in the 1960s his approval rating would have been well in excess of anything he enjoyed in his native USA. His famous visit to this country a few months before his assassination in Dallas copper-fastened Ireland's love affair with the man and his family.

He might well have decided that a brief stopover in Shannon was about the right amount of attention to devote to the political and economic backwater that his great-grandfather had abandoned in the 1850s. Instead, he chose to share four days with a smitten and adoring Irish public. When he, as a younger man, had tea with his distant cousins in Dunganstown, Co.Wexford, no one, perhaps not even the man himself, had expected that he would return as the 'leader of the free world'.

While he travelled in a triumphant motorcade through the streets of Dublin and became the first US President to address the Oireachtas, there is more than a sneaking suspicion that the part of the trip he enjoyed most was the time he spent in Wexford. Whether it was his second tea party in Dunganstown, the speech in New Ross, or laying a wreath at the memorial to Commodore John Barry, for twenty-four hours the returned native became one of the Boys of Wexford.

But the centrepiece of the visit was his address to both houses of the Oireachtas. It took place on 28 June 1963. Kennedy was introduced by the Ceann Comhairle Patrick Hogan. The President came bearing a significant gift, one of the flags of the 69th New York militia regiment, the so-called Fighting 69th of the Irish Brigade who suffered heavy casualties in the American Civil War.

Unfortunately, whoever researched his speech let the President down. He began with an error in the first sentence where he told his audience of TDs and Senators that the Civil War Battle of Fredericksburg had been fought in September 1862. It actually took place in December of that year.

This was followed by another howler in the second paragraph. Here he described the casualties of the Irish Brigade at Fredericksburg. Of the 1,200 men who went into battle, 280 survived. Fair enough so far, but he then went on to claim that the brigade had been led into battle by its commander, Brigadier General Thomas Francis Meagher. In fact, Meagher, who would normally have been at the head of his unit, had suffered an injury and took no part in the fighting.

He went on to redeem himself many times over with an inspiring speech that includes one of the lines most associated with him – though it's not actually his. Quoting George Bernard Shaw, he observed that 'Other people see things and say: "Why?" … But I dream things that never were – and I say: "Why not?" '

There was also one interesting postscript. In the course of his speech the President made a jocular reference to his distant namesake Lord Edward Fitzgerald, and his antipathy towards his

Fitzgerald family home, Leinster House. The 1798 rebel leader had once written to his mother, in a line quoted by Kennedy, 'Leinster House does not inspire the brightest ideas'. The quip caused offence to President Eamon de Valera who later, according to Taoiseach Sean Lemass, took issue with Kennedy and told him that he had done Irish politicians no service in cracking this particular joke. The sentiment, however, is arguably just as valid today as it was in 1963.

The remark is said to have been subsequently expunged from the Dáil record, but if that *was* the case, it has since been reinstated.

John Fitzgerald Kennedy, thirty-fifth President of the United States of America, began his state visit to Ireland, fifty-two years ago, on this day.

Broadcast 26 June 2015

July

Douglas "Wrong Way" Corrigan arrives on a West Coast

25 July 1633
Thomas, Viscount Wentworth,
Becomes Lord Deputy of Ireland

Thomas Wentworth, 1st Earl of Strafford, was a man who served his king, 'not wisely but too well'. The king in question was the hapless Charles I. The second Stuart king was perennially hard up and Wentworth, one of his most efficient and loyal ministers, made it his business to secure enough funds for whatever adventure in which his monarch wished to involve himself. This mostly meant beating off the attempts of Charles's unruly parliament to chip away at his power.

In 1632 Wentworth was despatched to Ireland as Lord Deputy. He was a capable administrator and made some significant changes in the governance of the country. As his primary objective was to make as much money out of Ireland as possible for the King so that he could govern without his irritating parliament, he made a number of Irish enemies. The worst of these was Richard Boyle, 1st Earl of Cork – and father of Robert Boyle, he of Boyle's Law fame.

Plain old Richard Boyle, born in England, had arrived in Ireland with twenty-seven pounds in his pocket in 1588. He married well and became tremendously rich tremendously quickly. Over the years he survived Irish rebellions, bankruptcy and various Irish and English plots against him. Cromwell once said of him, 'If there had been an Earl of Cork in every province it would have been impossible for the Irish to have raised a rebellion.' Thankfully there wasn't. But Boyle, like every self-respecting Corkman since, was not about to be pushed around. Not even by Wentworth.

But pushed around he certainly was, initially at least. Wentworth decided that Boyle stood in the way of his Irish plans and chose to humiliate him. In an exhibition of small-minded pettiness that would come back to bite the 1st Earl of Strafford, the great Earl of Cork was forced by Wentworth to remove the body of his wife from St Patrick's Cathedral. Boyle, however, was renowned for his capacity for deferred gratification. This meant he was well accustomed to wait in the long grass and when Wentworth fell afoul of Parliament, where he was impeached for 'high misdemeanours' after his return to England in 1639, Boyle was an enthusiastic witness against him at his trial.

King Charles, against his will, was forced to sign the Earl of Strafford's death warrant, pronouncing the immortal 'this hurts me more than it hurts you' line when he said 'My Lord Strafford's condition is happier than mine'. This was patently untrue at the time – the King wasn't going to lose his head – but it certainly was the case eight years later when Charles I himself faced the chop after Cromwell and Parliament decided that it was time to be rid of him too.

There are two versions of Wentworth's reaction when he received the news that he had been abandoned by the King and was to be executed – one account says he took the news well – another suggests that he reacted by saying, 'put not your trust in Princes'.

Wentworth's execution was said to have been witnessed by 300,000 souls, proof positive that if you give the people what they want they will turn up in droves. However, as the entire population of London at the time numbered about 300,000, the figure may be a little bit off, unless it was greatly swollen by an awful lot of curious out-of-towners. One of the witnesses, from a nearby rooftop, was the King. He is said to have fainted when the axe fell.

Richard Boyle wasn't there to gloat in person, but he wrote to a friend that Wentworth 'had his head struck off on Tower Hill, as he well deserved'. No trace of vindictiveness so.

Thomas Wentworth took up the office of Lord Deputy of Ireland, three hundred and eighty-one years ago, on this day.

Broadcast on 25 July 2014

24 July 1750
The Birth of Barrister and Politician
John Philpot Curran

On the morning of his fifty-third birthday, the leading Irish barrister of his day, John Philpot Curran, would have received news of serious disturbances in the city of Dublin. He would have been horrified to learn of the brutal death of his friend Lord Kilwarden, who was dragged from his coach along with his nephew and daughter and stabbed repeatedly with pikes.

However, the violence of 23 July 1803 was to come even closer to home for Curran. He would quickly have learned that it was no angry and leaderless mob that had murdered Kilwarden. It was the last throw of the dice of the United Irishmen, supposedly suppressed viciously five years earlier, in a rebellion led by a young Dublin Protestant, Robert Emmet. That name would come to haunt Curran.

John Philpot Curran was one of the most celebrated Irish public figures of his day. He was a politician, having been a member of the Irish parliament for three different constituencies. He was probably the most capable member of the Irish bar and had, in 1798, ably but futilely defended many of the leaders of the United Irishmen's rebellion. His early career as a barrister had been marred by a serious stammer that had earned him the unenviable nickname 'Stuttering Jack Curran'. But he had eventually conquered his disability, apparently by spending hours reciting Shakespeare in front of a mirror.

He was also a duellist, having fought up to half a dozen opponents and survived.

One of those encounters highlights his penchant for 'lost causes' or, at the very least, his affiliation with the underdog. In 1780, Curran, himself a wealthy and well-connected Protestant, took on the case of an elderly Catholic priest, Father Neale, who had fallen foul of a distinctly obnoxious aristocrat, Lord Doneraile. The priest had criticised the brother of Doneraile's mistress for maintaining an adulterous relationship and Doneraile, as you did if you were called – I kid you not – St Léger St Léger (his parents must have been extremely attached to the family name) had horsewhipped Father Neale for his croppy effrontery. St Léger (squared) did not anticipate a jury of his peers deciding to punish him, but he reckoned without Curran's powers of persuasion. The young advocate's arguments coaxed the jury into awarding the horsewhipped priest thirty guineas in damages and an affronted Doneraile challenged Curran to a duel. He fired and missed; Curran walked away without shooting.

While Curran may have opposed the Act of Union and defended the United Irishmen, his tolerance did not extend as far as permitting a relationship to form between his daughter Sarah and Robert Emmet. However, after the capture of the young rebel in the wake of his abortive *coup,* Curran agreed to defend Emmet. He was unaware, however, that his client and his daughter had been corresponding in secret. When the authorities came to search his house and he was apprised of the existence of letters between the young rebel and his youngest daughter, he threw up the brief. Crucially he was replaced as defence counsel by the Crown's most valuable intelligence asset in Dublin, the traitorous United Irishman Leonard McNally.

Curran was famous as a wit and phrasemaker. It may well have been he, rather than Edmund Burke, who uttered the immortal line 'evil prospers when good men do nothing'. He said of an enemy that 'his smile is like the silver plate on a coffin', and Karl Marx once advised Friedrich Engels to read Curran's speeches. In a mealtime encounter with the infamous Irish hanging judge, Lord Norbury, His Honour inquired of Curran if a particular piece of meat he was about to consume was 'hung-beef', to which Curran responded acidly 'Do try it my Lord, then it is sure to be'.

In his private life he was often unhappy. He disowned his daughter Sarah and later his wife, also called Sarah and with whom he had nine children, ran off with a Protestant rector whom Curran sued for criminal conversation. But as a public figure, Curran was a colossus who spanned the period between Henry Grattan and Daniel O'Connell and was, in many ways, the equal of both.

John Philpot Curran, scholar, poet, wit, barrister, politician, and humanitarian, was born two hundred and sixty-five years ago, on this day.

Broadcast 24 July 2015

11 July 1792
The Belfast Harp Festival Begins

Denis Hampson would have been a rarity in nineteenth-century Ireland if only for his longevity. He died in 1807 but he had been born in the seventeenth century, probably in 1695. He is, therefore, one of the few men to have lived through the eighteenth century in its entirety.

But Hampson has another claim to fame. He was one of the great practitioners of an ancient Irish art which was dying out as he drew his last breath in the year Napoleon first made war on Russia and the slave trade was abolished throughout the British Empire. Hampson was a harpist, a man who made his living collecting, composing and playing tunes for wealthy patrons.

What made his life even more extraordinary is that, like a number of the men who followed his trade, he had been blinded by smallpox at the age of three. Hampson was from the Magilligan area in Co. Derry and was first taught to play the harp by a woman named Bridget O'Cathain. He acquired a harp of his own at the age of eighteen and spent most of his twenties travelling and playing in Ireland and Scotland. Many years later, on a return trip to Scotland in 1745, he performed before Bonnie Prince Charlie, the pretender Charles Stuart. His harp, which became known as the Downhill harp after his last patron, Frederick Hervey, 4th Earl of Bristol and Bishop of Derry, who built the Downhill estate, is on display at the Guinness hop-store in Dublin, having been bought by the company in the 1960s.

Hampson was also notorious for a swelling or a 'wen' on the back of his head. In 1805, when he was more than one hundred years old, Hampson was visited by the Rev. George Vaughan Sampson of Magilligan who wrote that 'the wen on the back of his head is greatly increased; it is now hanging over his neck and shoulders, nearly as large as his head'. Towards the end of his life Hampson was actually nicknamed 'the man with two heads'.

He married, at the age of eighty-six, a lady described only as 'a woman from Inishowen', by whom he had a daughter and several grandchildren. Hampson once said of the marriage: 'I can't tell if it was not the devil buckled us together, she being lame and I blind'.

In 1792, at the age of ninety-six, Hampson was prevailed upon to attend the Belfast Harper's Assembly, organised by, among others, United Irishman Henry Joy McCracken. It was the first such assembly for six years. A young Edward Bunting, who would go on to collect and record hundreds of traditional tunes, was engaged to notate the music played by the one Welsh and ten Irish harpers who gathered for the festival. Hampson was described as playing with long, crooked fingernails.

Hampson was not a fan of the most celebrated Irish harpist and composer of harp music, Turlough O'Carolan from Co. Meath. While much of O'Carolan's repertoire was featured at the Belfast Harper's Assembly, Hampson himself resolutely refused to perform the work of his great and more famous contemporary.

Denis Hampson graced the Belfast Harper's Assembly with his presence at the tender age of ninety-six. The festival began two hundred and twenty-two years ago, on this day.

Broadcast 11 July 2014

18 July 1822
The New Theatre Royal Opens in Dublin

Like the famed Horsemen of the Apocalypse, there have been not one but four Theatre Royal establishments in Dublin since the first incarnation opened in Smock Alley in 1662. In the eighteenth century the original version was managed by Thomas Sheridan, father of the playwright Richard Brinsley Sheridan, who proved his Colganesque powers of persuasion by enticing the likes of David Garrick and Peg Woffington over to Dublin to perform.

That manifestation of the Theatre Royal closed in 1787. It wasn't until 1822 that another theatre of the same name opened in Hawkins Street. It had two thousand seats and cost a gargantuan £50,000 to build. Its first claim to fame was that it became the scene of one of the most famous riots in a Dublin theatre – coming a decent third after the Abbey's *Playboy of the Western World* disturbances of 1907 and the *Plough and the Stars* convulsions of 1926.

This particular flap has gone down in history as 'The Bottle Riot'. It happened in December 1822 and was sparked by the perception that the Lord Lieutenant, Marquess Wellesley – brother of the Duke of Wellington – was insufficiently interested in keeping Roman Catholics in their proper place, as second class citizens. A disaffected spectator, spotting the Viceroy in his box, threw a bottle and then a rattle at Wellesley – presumably the latter projectile had come from his own pram. As a result, fighting broke out among the Orange and Green members of the audience. For the record, the play on stage, which became a bit of an irrelevance really, was Goldsmith's wonderful *She Stoops To Conquer*. This was, in effect, how the Lord Lieutenant chose to react to the missile attack. In a bit of an over-reaction for the assault on his exalted personage, he had three of the rioters charged with conspiracy to murder. As juries in Dublin at the time were overwhelmingly unionist, the charges did not stick.

Before Theatre Royal Mark Two burned to the ground in 1880 it had hosted, among others, Paganini, Jenny Lynd and the original Tyrone Power.

TR3 opened in 1897 on the site of its cremated predecessor – it too had a seating capacity of over two thousand. One of its claims to fame was that, in 1906, a young Charlie Chaplin performed there as part of an act called 'The Eight Lancashire Lads'. The other seven have never been heard of since. The building was demolished in 1934.

The fourth Theatre Royal – the final horseman, was an impressive art deco building which could house almost four thousand paying patrons. Unfortunately, it did not do so with sufficient regularity. It was at a disadvantage because of its size and struggled because of the lively competition from the nearby Gaiety and Olympia Theatres. One of its most famous fixtures was its dance troupe, the Royalettes. Despite attracting international acts of the calibre of Gracie Fields, Jimmy Durante, George Formby, Max Wall and Judy Garland – and despite doubling as a cinema – the theatre found it hard to make ends meet.

The fourth and final Theatre Royal finally closed its doors in 1962, three hundred years after its Smock Alley incarnation. The magnificent art deco building was demolished and replaced by the magnificent multi-storey office block Hawkins House, home to our magnificent Department of Health.

The second Theatre Royal opened its doors, one hundred and ninety-two years ago, on this day.

Broadcast 18 July 2014

4 July 1836
The Establishment of the
Dublin Metropolitan Police

From the perspective of Irish nationalists, the Dublin Metropolitan Police, despite its well-publicised excesses during the 1913 Lockout, has a more benign reputation than it's fraternal force, the Royal Irish Constabulary. The DMP, established in 1836, was based on a template devised by Sir Robert Peel for the London Metropolitan Police – also known, for that reason, as the Peelers. The force was unarmed and was not disbanded until 1925 – three years after Irish independence.

DMP men, mostly from rural Ireland, worked hard for their pay and pension. They put in fifty-six hours a week, and were armed only with a truncheon. Most were extremely tall by comparison with the undersized Dubliners of the slums it fell to them to patrol. Between 1836 and 1925 more than twelve thousand men served in the DMP, with its normal complement being just over one thousand at any one time.

Probably the most famous member of the DMP was Superintendent John Mallon from Co. Armagh. Mallon rose up through the ranks to lead the elite 'G' Division of the force in the 1880s. Their main interest was in political crime and, what we would call today, counter terrorism.

It was Mallon who played a huge part in identifying the members of the Invincibles, the shadowy revolutionary organisation who were responsible for the murders in Phoenix Park in May 1882 of the newly appointed Chief Secretary Lord Frederick Cavendish and Under Secretary Thomas H. Burke. Mallon broke the case with an inspired piece of subterfuge. Two of the chief suspects, both of whom, as it happened, had actually been directly involved in the killings, were Dubliners Daniel Curley and James Carey, the latter being recently elected to the City Council. Mallon had a feeling that Carey might try and save his own skin if confronted with the probability of execution. When a number of the murder suspects were rounded up, he arranged that Carey be placed in a cell in Kilmainham Gaol and that the cell next door be left empty. The reasons for this soon became clear.

After Carey was incarcerated, he must have become aware of a procession of well-known policemen and legal figures trooping in and out of the neighbouring cell. Carey, of course, had no idea that it was vacant. He quickly came to the conclusion that whoever was next door had done a deal with the Crown and was turning State's evidence in the Phoenix Park case. That would not be good news for Carey. He nonchalantly inquired of a prison guard who it was who occupied the cell next door. Of course the guard had been primed by Mallon to tell him that it was Daniel Curley. This confirmed Carey's worst fears: Curley had informed. Speed was of the essence. He had to offer his information before Curley's evidence was accepted and he was given immunity. Carey immediately asked to speak to Mallon and his testimony was used to hang five of the members of the Invincibles.

Although Mallon's Catholicism and his usefulness as head of 'G' Division made it difficult for him to rise above the rank of Superintendent, he retired in 1901, as an Assistant Commissioner of the force.

The Dublin Metropolitan Police was established, one hundred and seventy-eight years ago, on this day.

Broadcast on 4 July 2014

10 July 1867
The Birth of Irish-American Satirist and Journalist Finlay Peter Dunne

For more than a decade, an irascible bartender from Roscommon, owner of a saloon in Chicago, became the most famous fictional character in American journalism. The bartender in question, a Mr Dooley, was the creation of the Irish-American humourist Finley Peter Dunne. Every week, in the pages of numerous newspapers across the USA, Dooley would hold forth on matters of public and domestic policy to Hennessy, his long-suffering customer, in an Irish dialect that often has to be read aloud to be properly understood.

Finley Peter Dunne was born in Chicago in 1867, the son of Irish immigrants who came to America as refugees from the Great Famine. He was brought up in the Irish neighbourhood of Bridgeport and began working for Chicago newspapers straight out of high school. In his mid-twenties he started composing Dooley's satirical monologues for the *Chicago Sunday Evening Post*. Many of Dooley's political views would not have been shared by his author. A latter-day version of Dooley, therefore, might be TV's Comedy Central creation Stephen Colbert.

Mr Dooley was never shy about expressing his opinions. In, for example, a column about the vexed topic of immigration (and remember this was the 1890s), Dooley, himself an immigrant, favours the lowering of the portcullis to prevent the entry of further migrants to the USA. Dooley tells Hennessy, whose own cousin is due to arrive in Chicago shortly that:

> *Tis time we put our back agin' the open door an' kept out th' savage horde. If that cousin of yers expects to cross, he'd better tear for th' ship. In a few minutes th' gates will be down an' when th' oppressed world comes hikin' acrost to th' haven of refuge, th' Goddess of Liberty will meet them at th' dock with an axe in her hand.*

Dunne coined a host of well-known aphorisms that have entered the great American lexicon, phrases such as 'Trust everyone, but cut the cards', 'The past only looks pleasant because it isn't here', 'Larceny is the sincerest form of flattery', and his pithy appraisal of corrupt, big-city politics, 'A vote on the tallysheet is worth two in the box'. He may also have coined the famous truism, 'All politics are local', an observation usually ascribed to the late Speaker of the House of Representatives, Tip O'Neill.

Perhaps Dooley's most pointed observation concerned Dunne's own profession. He once said of the newspaper business that:

> *The newspaper does ivrything for us. It runs th' polis foorce an' th' banks, commands th' milishy, controls th' ligislachure, baptizes th' young, marries th' foolish, comforts th' afflicted, afflicts th' comfortable, buries th' dead an' roasts thim aftherward.*

The reference to comforting the afflicted and afflicting the comfortable has been adopted and claimed as a mantra by many journalists, writers and activists.

Despite the numerous barbs aimed at his administration, President Theodore Roosevelt contrived to be on very friendly terms with Dunne. Roosevelt would regularly read out Dunne's columns at Cabinet meetings to alert the nation's political leaders to the *vox populi* – Dooley being seen as a man of the people and reflecting the opinions of the man on the street.

Dunne, in 1902, married one Margaret Ives Abbot, who just happened to be the first American woman to have won an Olympic gold medal. She was the women's golf champion at the 1900 Paris Olympiad. In 1910, after writing more than seven hundred columns, Dunne ended the career of the garrulous Roscommon bartender and no more was heard from Mr Dooley.

Irish-American writer, Finlay Peter Dunne, humourist, journalist and one of America's most successful newspaper columnists, was born, one hundred and forty-eight years ago, on this day.

Broadcast 10 July 2015

3 July 1878
The Birth of Irish-American
Performer and Composer
George M. Cohan

The chorus goes:

> *I'm a Yankee Doodle Dandy,*
> *A Yankee Doodle, do or die;*
> *A real live nephew of my Uncle Sam,*
> *Born on the Fourth of July.*

Sadly, however, for the sake of symmetry and posterity, the real-life Yankee Doodle Dandy who composed that song was actually born on 3 July.

The song and dance man, who went on to become one of the most popular vaudeville singers and composers of *his* generation, and a few others besides, was born George Michael Cohan of Irish parents in Providence, Rhode Island, in 1878. His family always insisted that he was actually born on American Independence Day, but the only available documentation suggests otherwise.

His kin were the Osmonds or the Jacksons of their day. Everybody was involved in the family business, a travelling vaudeville act, and young George first trod the boards as an infant.

Legend has it that he learned to sing and dance shortly after he learned to walk. He was certainly performing by the age of eight as part of the Four Cohans, with Mum, Dad and sister Josie. He was already writing sketches and songs for the act while still only in his teens. He sold his first songs to a publisher at the age of fifteen and in 1904 – still only twenty-six – he had his first huge commercial success in the musical *Little Johnny Jones,* which included the massive hit tunes 'Give My Regards to Broadway' and the aforementioned 'Yankee Doodle Boy' – later made even more famous by James Cagney in the film based on Cohan's life, *Yankee Doodle Dandy,* for which Cagney won an Oscar for Best Actor.

Little Johnny Jones is based on the life of American jockey Tod Sloan who rode the King's horse in the 1903 Derby. Cohan amply established his patriotic Irish-American credentials with a line in the musical given to the lead character. It goes: 'You think I'd marry an heiress and live off her money? What do you take me for? An Englishman?'

Between 1904 and 1920 Cohan was responsible for over twenty musicals, plays and revues on Broadway. His shows often ran simultaneously in four or five theatres. As a so-called 'Tin Pan Alley' composer – the name derives from the New York street that housed many of the music publishing companies – he also wrote over three hundred hit tunes for himself and other recording artists.

Cohan also appeared in many 'straight' acting roles, most notably in the Eugene O'Neill play *Ah Wilderness.*

While he seriously antagonised many colleagues in the acting profession by opposing a major Actors Equity strike in 1919 – he was also a producer and so had a foot in both camps – he compensated to some extent by scoring a major victory for his acting peers over the US Internal Revenue Service. He forced the IRS to concede that he, and others like him, should be allowed to deduct travel and entertainment expenses from their tax returns. This has since become known as the 'Cohan clause'.

The composer claimed that one of his best-known songs, 'Over There', was written on a short train journey after he heard that the USA had entered the First World War. The song finishes with the famous line, 'And we won't come back till it's over, over there'. The final line of the song was appropriately adapted by American soldiers in Europe to read, 'And we won't come back, we'll be buried over there'. It is better known today for its use in a TV advertisement by a price comparison website – voted the most irritating commercial on television in 2009 and 2010.

George M.Cohan, the greatest Irish-American vaudeville artist of them all, prodigious composer, and the only actor to have his statue erected on Broadway, was born one hundred and thirty-seven years ago, on this day.

Broadcast 3 July 2015

17 July 1938
Transatlantic Pilot Douglas 'Wrong Way' Corrigan Takes Off from New York

In the early hours of 18 July 1938 a rather flimsy, sorry-looking, and frankly jerry-built plane landed at Baldonnel Aerodrome. Its arrival had not been expected, and the authorities at the airport were astonished to discover that its pilot, thirty-one-year-old Douglas Corrigan, casually claimed to have just flown from New York.

Corrigan, a Texan of Irish descent, was a pilot and engineer who had worked with the Ryan Aeronautical Company on the construction of Charles Lindbergh's *Spirit of St Louis*. This was the plane that, in 1927, made the first non-stop solo flight from New York to Paris. Corrigan had made his own first solo flight in 1926 and had become severely bitten by the flying bug.

He quickly graduated to stunt flying, much to the annoyance of his employers at the Airtech Flying School in San Diego, whose planes he was jeopardising. Corrigan paid no attention to their disapproval, simply taking their planes to a more distant aerodrome and performing stunts during his lunch hour, unseen by his bosses. As we shall see, the watchword for Corrigan seems to have been 'out of sight out of mind'.

In 1933 he spent three hundred dollars on a four-year-old Curtiss Robin monoplane and started to modify it. To put this into some perspective, *Spirit of St Louis* cost more than ten thousand dollars to build. Corrigan had decided he wanted to emulate Lindbergh, but he was going to target his ancestral home, Ireland, as his destination.

When he applied for a licence to make the trip in 1935 he was turned down on the not unreasonable basis that his plane was a glorified wreck incapable of surviving the trip. No amount of modifications over two years would make the authorities change their minds.

From California, Corrigan flew his plane across the USA in July 1938, barely making it to New York before a gasoline leak got him first. He then filed a flight plan for a return trip to the West Coast. He took off on 17 July at 5.15 a.m., but instead of turning west he headed east. He claimed afterwards that low cloud and a faulty compass had brought about the slight error that took him out over the Atlantic. Nobody believed him. Most people who knew him were aware of his obsession.

Twenty-eight hours and thirteen minutes after take-off, Corrigan landed at Baldonnel. He had survived on two bars of chocolate and two fig bars; he had to get his bearings by leaning out of the side of his airplane; – he had placed his fuel tanks in front of the cockpit – he had no radio and only a twenty-year-old compass for navigation, which he almost certainly didn't bother to read until he knew he was over the Atlantic and not New Jersey.

An American journalist with the delightful name of H. R. Knickerbocker, who interviewed Corrigan in Ireland after his epic journey, wrote three years later that:

> *You may say that Corrigan's flight could not be compared to Lindbergh's in its sensational appeal as the first solo flight across the ocean. Yes, but in another way the obscure little Irishman's flight was the more audacious of the two. Lindbergh had a plane specially constructed, the finest money could buy. He had*

lavish financial backing, friends to help him at every turn. Corrigan had nothing but his own ambition, courage, and ability. His plane, a nine-year-old Curtiss Robin, was the most wretched-looking jalopy.

Corrigan's 'mistake' might not have gone down well in official aviation circles – his licence was suspended for fourteen days and his hero Charles Lindbergh never acknowledged his achievement – but he was a big hit with the general public and returned to a hero's welcome in the USA. He received a ticker tape parade in New York, which, apparently, was attended by more people than greeted Lindbergh. Later he starred in a movie about his own life called *The Flying Irishman,* delighted in the nickname 'Wrong Way Corrigan' and endorsed numerous appropriate products, such as a watch that told the time backwards.

Douglas 'Wrong-Way' Corrigan took off from New York, bound for California but got conveniently lost along the way, seventy-seven years ago, on this day.

Broadcast 17 July 2015

31 July 1917
The Death of Meath-Born Poet
Francis Ledwidge in the Great War

He shall not hear the bittern cry
In the wild sky where he is lain.
Nor voices of the sweeter birds
Above the wailing of the rain.

So begins a poem most Irish schoolchildren of a certain age would have learned off by heart, a short elegy for the executed 1916 leader Thomas MacDonagh, written by his friend and fellow nationalist Francis Ledwidge.

What makes those poignant and beautiful lines all the more interesting is that they were written by a man whose daily attire, at the time of writing, was British khaki. Ledwidge was serving with the Inniskilling Fusiliers when he wrote his stirring farewell to MacDonagh. The lines do not reflect the bitterness Ledwidge felt at his own predicament, as an Irish nationalist in a Manchester hospital recovering from wounds incurred on behalf of the government and the army; the same government and army that had shot his fellow poet out of hand after the dismal failure of the Easter Rising.

How did pastoral poet Francis Ledwidge, son of a Slane, Co. Meath labourer, end up fighting with the British army in Gallipoli in 1915 and later in the brutal Ypres sector of the Western Front? He had been encouraged in his writing by the Unionist peer Lord Dunsany. It is widely assumed that he was also persuaded by Dunsany to follow him into the armed forces. The truth is rather more complex.

Ledwidge was what was often called at the time an 'advanced nationalist'. He was a Republican who sided with the minority section of the Irish Volunteers of Eoin MacNeill, Padráig Pearse and Thomas MacDonagh in 1914 after the organisation split in the wake of John Redmond's call to Irishmen to go 'wherever the firing line extends' in the Great War.

Ledwidge thus allied himself with the faction opposed to Irish enlistment in the British army but still joined the 5th Inniskilling Fusiliers. He did so out of a horror of German militarism, a romantic disappointment – the love of his life, Ellie Vaughey, had married another man – and the taunts of Remondite fellow councillors on the Navan rural district council who upbraided him for his anti-militarist stance. His riposte to the Redmondites was to observe that 'I joined the British army because she stood between Ireland and an enemy common to our civilisation and I would not have her say that she defended us while we did nothing at home but pass resolutions'.

Political disillusionment following the Easter Rising and the torment of his war experience led to a serious drinking problem – hardly unique on the Western front in 1917. Ledwidge, a lance corporal, was once court-martialled and lost his stripe after an altercation with another soldier about the Easter Rising.

While he died in the course of the extended and bloody battle of Passchendaele, he was not the direct victim of one of the many futile assaults into no-man's-land ordered by British generals, who lost four hundred thousand men in five months between July and November 1917. He was simply killed by a random shell during a lull in the fighting.

Ledwidge is buried in Artillery Wood cemetery north of Ypres – a short distance away, in the same cemetery, is his Welsh contemporary, Ellis Humphrey Evans, or the lyric poet Hedd Wynn – a year apart in age, they died on the same day.

On Ledwidge's memorial stone in Slane, the Thomas MacDonagh poem is inscribed. A more appropriate poem might have been 'A Soldier's Grave' from his posthumous *Last Songs*, published in 1918.

> *Then in the lull of midnight, gentle arms*
> *Lifted him slowly down the slopes of death,*
> *Lest he should hear again the mad alarms*
> *Of battle, dying moans, and painful breath.*
>
> *And where the earth was soft for flowers we made*
> *A grave for him that he might better rest.*
> *So, Spring shall come and leave it sweet arrayed,*
> *And there the lark shall turn her dewy nest.*

Francis Ledwidge, 'poet of the blackbirds', trade unionist, national-ist and infantryman, died ninety-eight years ago, on this day.

Broadcast 31 July 2015

August

The 'local Newspaper effect'

15 August 1649
Oliver Cromwell Arives in Ireland

Some visitors are welcome, some are unwelcome, and then there is that small cohort whose members are so unwelcome as to make all previous undesirables seem like fragrant blossoms on a spring day.

Ireland had already hosted the Normans, a few underemployed English kings like John and Richard II, the zealots of the Reformation and an unsuccessful adventure by one of Queen Elizabeth I's boyfriends – sorry … alleged boyfriends.

But the prize for the least welcome visitor to Ireland since the Bubonic Plague in the fifteenth century undoubtedly went to Oliver Cromwell, who made the crossing in 1649. In England he may well be the great Lord Protector and progenitor of British democracy. In Ireland he's an ethnic cleanser, genocidal military commander and all-round bad guy.

A slight caveat. In the interests of balance and fair play it should be pointed out that there are some historians who believe the extent of Cromwell's depredations in Ireland are exaggerated. To others he was a product of his times who was merely avenging the slaughter of Protestants by rebellious Catholics in 1641.

In the lobby of the Reform Club in London, Cromwell's status in the UK is recognised by a distinctive bust presented to this Liberal bastion in 1864. Interestingly, just across the hallway, is a portrait of another great British Liberal hero, the Irishman Daniel O'Connell. It must be exquisite torture for both men to be placed in such juxtaposition and to have to eyeball each other every day of every year for the foreseeable future. O'Connell must look at Cromwell's bust, 'warts and all' and see the image of the man who ravaged the Catholic population of Ireland with his Parliamentary Roundhead armies. Cromwell, on the other hand, must seethe at the sight of the man who became the first Catholic to take a seat in his precious House of Commons. That's if busts and paintings could talk. Which of course they can't. Shame really.

Cromwell arrived in this country to take his turn at putting manners on the rowdy Irish as Commander-in-Chief of an army of twenty thousand men. He is not remembered fondly in Drogheda where, after taking the town, his soldiers were permitted to slaughter the inhabitants. His celebrated New Model Army – not so described because its members were ideal role models – then went south and did the same in Wexford.

By the time Cromwell had finished his self-appointed task, the population of Ireland had declined by anything between twenty to fifty per cent. When he had finished killing and confiscating, Cromwell rounded up an additional fifty thousand or so unfortunates and despatched them into slavery.

The so-called Cromwellian Settlement was the most efficient and comprehensive land grab in Irish history. Many of Cromwell's soldiers were paid with the land over which they fought. Think of the seventeenth-century equivalent of a leveraged buy-out where you use the assets of the company you want to purchase to acquire the money to buy it. Manchester United fans, however, should be careful not to compare the acquisition of their club by the Glazers to the Cromwellian plantation of Ireland.

Oliver Cromwell arrived in this country with the catchy slogan, 'To Hell or to Connaught' on his lips and revenge in his heart, three hundred and sixty-five years ago, on this day.

Broadcast 15 August 2014

29 August 1729
The Birth of Banker
David La Touche

Today the tale of a banker who didn't manage to destroy the country while in pursuit of a fat bonus.

David La Touche, born in 1729, was the grandson of a Huguenot officer in the army of William of Orange. La Touche married the cousin of Henry Grattan, the great eighteenth-century Irish politician and the man who had a parliament named after him, though it didn't even last twenty years. Elizabeth Marlay – Mrs. La Touche – is unwittingly remembered today by thousands of Dubliners who live near the park in Rathfarnham that is called after her. This was actually the home of the La Touche family for many years. Its grounds were laid out by David La Touche in the 1760s.

The house is modest enough by the standards of the day – it would merely be an annexe of Carton or Castletown – but it did have its own private theatre. There, Henry Grattan and Henry Flood, champions of the quasi-independent Irish parliament of the late eighteenth century, once performed in Shakespeare's *Macbeth*. Their involvement in a production of the infamous 'Scottish play' – bringer of bad luck to all who perform in her – may well have contributed to the Act of Union that saw their grand project go the way of the dinosaur and the dodo.

Despite having married Grattan's relative, La Touche had no qualms in voting for the abolition of Cousin Henry's Patriot parliament. He was one of three La Touche brothers to sit in the Irish parliament. The others voted against the Act of Union. Many of those who supported the abolition of the Irish parliament were rewarded with large sums of money and posh titles, or at least posher titles than the ones they had already. After 1800, La Touche was still plain old David La Touche, so he might well have voted to abolish the College Green parliament based on, shockingly, political conviction. He would also have been difficult to bribe as by then he didn't need the money.

The lack of need for money was because he ran the family bank for a number of years. The La Touche bank had been established by David's father, also called David La Touche – they weren't very imaginative when it came to first names, possibly because the surname was more than sufficiently exotic for eighteenth-century Ireland. The family bank was one of the few such institutions to survive a serious financial crisis in the 1750s. In the late nineteenth century it had the misfortune to be merged with the Munster Bank. Just over a decade later the Munster Bank – a forerunner of AIB – went bust while under the guardianship of the former politician William Shaw. But David La Touche also swam in the gene pool that became the Bank of Ireland. In 1783 he helped to draft the charter of the Bank of Ireland, in which his family initially held a major shareholding – nothing like Sean Quinn in Anglo of course, but just under ten per cent nonetheless.

La Touche was also Deputy Grand Master of the Freemasons and not a fan of Catholic Emancipation. He voted against giving Catholics the vote in 1793.

David La Touche III, banker, politician and mason, was born two hundred and eighty-five years ago, on this day.

Broadcast 29 August 2014

8 August 1781
The First Stone is Laid at the Site the Custom House in Dublin

It's odd to think that when the architect James Gandon moved from London to Dublin, the largest city in Ireland was also one of the largest in Europe. It was far from the political and economic backwater it became after that other 'Flight of the Earls' – in this case Anglo-Irish aristocrats – in the aftermath of the passage of the Act of Union and the dissolution of the Irish parliament in 1800.

Gandon first come to prominence by finishing second. In 1769, at the age of twenty-six, he had entered a competition to design the new Royal Exchange in Dublin. In case you're scratching your head wondering 'where is the Royal Exchange in Dublin?', we call it City Hall these days. That competition was won by another British architect who settled in Ireland, Thomas Cooley.

Gandon may have been unlucky on that occasion, but he was much more fortunate in 1780 when Cooley, who was supposed to be responsible for the building of the Custom House, died suddenly before work had begun. Gandon was asked to step in and complete the job. He turned down a commission from a member of the Russian Royal family to take on the challenge.

The Romanov's loss was Dublin's gain. However, the population of the city would not have seen it that way at the time.

The Custom House, which many Dubliners alleged was being built on a swamp, was the pet project of John Beresford, the most powerful aristocrat in Ireland in the late eighteenth century. Beresford could, more or less, ram through whatever project he wanted, but that didn't make them popular with the taxpayers who had to foot the bill.

In order to avoid Gandon becoming collateral damage, Beresford smuggled him into the country and put him up in his own house until the building was well under way and the project unstoppable. The eventual bill – footed by the taxpayers of course – was two hundred thousand pounds – that's around forty million euros in today's money.

From 1780 to 1800 Dublin grew to be the fifth largest city in Europe, and Beresford and Gandon were at the heart of many of the fine buildings that were constructed during that time. For a follow up to the Custom House, Gandon designed the Four Courts – where, presumably, taxpayers who hadn't stumped up for the Custom House could be indicted and jailed. Gandon also worked for the Wide Streets Commissioners in developing the cityscape with which we are familiar today.

Gandon also designed a number of private dwellings, the most notable of these are Emo Court in Co. Laois and Abbeville in North Dublin. The latter was the country home of Beresford but a couple of centuries later it was acquired by another equally powerful Irish political figure, Charles J. Haughey.

Despite the impressive architectural legacy he left behind, Gandon was never popular while he worked in Dublin. His costly public buildings were resented by those who had to pay for their construction. He was frequently lambasted in the largely unionist press of the day. When the 1798 rebellion broke out Gandon figured he might become the victim of some nifty work with a pike and fled to London.

He eventually did come back and died in his house in Lucan in 1823. But the city he had helped to create was slowly destroyed by the Act of Union and the loss of the Irish parliament. By the end of the nineteenth century it had been surpassed in population and wealth by Belfast. It is ironic that his two great creations survived the animosity of the late eighteenth century, only to be destroyed in the revolutionary period of the early 1920's.

The first stone was laid on the Custom House site, two hundred and thirty-three years ago, on this day.

Broadcast 8 August 2014

14 August 1814
The Birth of Mary O'Connell,
'The American Florence Nightingale'

A 2003 US Defence Department report makes reference to the emergency medical procedures instituted by a nurse which, in the words of the Pentagon, 'remain standard practice in every theatre of war where American troops fight'. One might be forgiven for assuming that these triage techniques were established during the Vietnam War, or maybe as far back as World War Two.

In fact, this medical innovator was a middle-aged Irishwoman who nursed Yankees and Rebels alike during the American Civil War. It seems that no one has radically improved on the sensible but revolutionary life-saving techniques she devised more than a century and a half ago. So, American soldiers wounded in Iraq and Afghanistan owe Limerickwoman Mary O'Connell an enormous debt of gratitude.

She was born a year before the Battle of Waterloo, in 1814, and left Limerick for Boston with her parents when she was just seven years old. Tragically, a few years after her arrival in the USA, she lost her mother.

In 1835 Mary O'Connell became a member of the American Sisters of Charity and took the name of Sister Anthony. Based in Cincinnati, Ohio at the outbreak of the Civil War, she immediately volunteered her services as a nurse.

Her kindly face was probably the last human contact for thousands of unfortunate victims of the internecine strife of the American Civil War. Her reputation as 'the angel of the battlefield' and the 'Florence Nightingale of America' was gained on the notorious killing fields of Cumberland Gap, Murfreesboro, Lynchburg and many others, but particularly at the Battle of Shiloh in April 1862. At this battle, thousands of Union and Confederate soldiers were killed or wounded in a single day. She arranged for injured soldiers to be evacuated to hospital ships on the nearby Tennessee river.

Her methods of dealing with seriously injured and dying men developed rapidly and gave her an authority not normally afforded to civilians, and especially not to women, in a military environment. Her interventions often saved the limbs of young men who would have become amputees had she not offered alternative treatments.

She was renowned for making no distinction between Union or Confederate, white or black soldiers; as a consequence, she was often left to treat prisoners of war. Her egalitarian attitude may have been influenced by her early upbringing in Boston. She lived in the city's North End – an ethnic Irish neighbourhood that was periodically raided and vandalised by Yankee mobs. On one occasion they burned to the ground the Ursuline convent where she was receiving an excellent education. While her work was praised by Abraham Lincoln, she was also on good terms, after the war, with the Confederate President Jefferson Davis, and was acquainted with generals on both sides of the conflict.

O'Connell also persuaded the American Roman Catholic Church to train more nuns like herself in nursing practice and allow them to use their newly-acquired skills on the battlefield. Assigned to a hospital in Nashville, she not only treated wounded soldiers but also runaway slaves suffering from smallpox.

After the Civil War she returned to Cincinnati and continued to work as a nurse, helped found a hospital and played a huge part in the suppression of a yellow fever epidemic in the city in 1877. She died in 1897.

Mary Murphy O'Connell, 'America's Florence Nightingale', was born in Limerick, two hundred and one years ago, on this day.

Broadcast 14 August 2015

28 August 1814
The Birth of Sheridan Le Fanu,
Writer of Gothic Fiction

The name Le Fanu doesn't sound particularly Irish. And that's because it's not particularly Irish. But one of the most celebrated gentlemen of that name definitely was.

Sheridan Le Fanu, born in Dublin in 1814, was of Huguenot descent. He was the son of a frequently impoverished clergyman and the grand-nephew of the great Irish playwright Richard Brinsley Sheridan, from whom he derived his Christian name. His father had the misfortune to be a Church of Ireland clergyman during the Tithe War, a time when Protestant rectors were about as welcome in most Irish rural communities as President Barack Obama at a Ku Klux Klan rally.

Le Fanu junior went to Trinity College where he became auditor of the Historical Society, the famous TCD debating forum. He began contributing stories to the *Dublin University Magazine* in 1838 and in 1840 became, for a short period, part owner of the Unionist newspaper the *Dublin Evening Mail*, which, many years after his tenure, would compare the Irish Land League to the Colorado Beetle.

Le Fanu's own political instincts were not quite as Tory as his shareholding in the *Mail* would suggest. During the Famine he allied himself to the likes of John Mitchel, Thomas Francis Meagher, Samuel Ferguson and Isaac Butt in condemning British policy in Ireland throughout the Famine years.

Le Fanu would become the leading writer of Gothic fiction in early Victorian Britain, the precursor of authors such as fellow Dubliner Bram Stoker. His ghostly creations may well have emerged from the horrors of the Great Famine and/or from tragedies closer to home. His wife Susanna suffered from mental illness and died in April 1858 after what was described as an 'hysterical attack'. After her death Le Fanu became almost a recluse.

Le Fanu's first great Gothic novel, *The House by the Churchyard*, published in 1863, is set in the Phoenix Park and Chapelizod and was used by James Joyce as a source for *Finnegans Wake*. Thereafter, however, for commercial reasons, his work was mostly set in England. In 1864 he had huge success with *Uncle Silas*, a mystery novel that influenced writers like Arthur Conan Doyle and Wilkie Collins. Two film versions have been made of the novel. His other outstanding success was *Carmilla*, a vampire novella set in Eastern Europe with a lesbian subtext that has inspired several films and certainly helped Stoker to write *Dracula*.

Le Fanu's plots include the aforementioned vampire, a man returning from the grave to claim his bride, a Faustian pact, Gothic castles, supernatural visitors and sundry other joyous subject matter. Like many other Irish writers, he also pillaged the Irish folk tradition with gusto, and to excellent effect. In this context it is odd that his first published story, 'The Ghost and the Bonesetter', is a comic narrative. He didn't persist with the genre.

Many of his short stories, which tend to be more Irish than his longer fiction, purport to be from the memoirs of an eighteenth-century Irish priest, Father Purcell. These were published in the *Dublin University Magazine* and often later mined by the author himself for the storylines of his novels.

Le Fanu might have produced even greater work and been remembered in the manner of Stoker, Edgar Allen Poe and Mary Shelley had his life been longer, but he died in 1873 at the age of fifty-nine.

Sheridan Le Fanu, ghost-writer in the traditional sense of the word, was born two hundred and one years ago, on this day.

Broadcast 28 August 2015

2 August 1855
The Annual Donnybrook Fair Comes to an End

Today it's a chic boutique supermarket in the suburbs of Dublin, but for six hundred and fifty-one years Donnybrook Fair was a different kind of market altogether, one better known for hooliganism than hummus, gangsterism than gazpacho.

It all began in 1204 when the much-unloved King John of England granted a licence to the Corporation of Dublin to hold an eight-day fair in Donnybrook, a few miles from the city. Doubtless the licence cost the city fathers a few bob as King John often found himself a wee bit short on account of the wars he was fighting to regain the family inheritance in France.

In 1252 the duration of the licence was extended from eight to fifteen days. Over the years, however, as the nature of the event changed, residents of the area couldn't wait to see the back of it. The fair graduated from a market to a fourteen-day bacchanalian orgy. It was a site not just for trade and commerce but for public entertainment and even more public drinking. By the eighteenth century, Donnybrook Fair had become a byword for violence, drunkenness and faction fighting. It was an Irish cliché.

In fact the word Donnybrook itself actually developed into a cliché, though not in this country. It is used in American political journalism to describe a metaphorical pitched battle between political opponents, generally at Presidential selection conventions. It's highly probable that most of the journalists who described, for example, the infamous 1968 Democratic Party Convention in Chicago as a 'donnybrook' had no clue as to the origins of the word.

The scenes of violence and drunken behaviour that characterised Donnybrook Fair would have been enacted on what has since become the Leinster Rugby Grounds – so nothing new there.

By the nineteenth century the campaign to bring an end to this annual fortnight of boozing and bare-knuckle fighting had taken wing. The Committee for the Abolition of Donnybrook Fair was established. The problem was that someone, somewhere, at some time, had secured for themselves the licence to stage the fair on an annual basis. For example, by the middle of the eighteenth century it was in the hands of one Henry Ussher, scion of the family who owned Donnybrook Castle. When he died in 1756 it was passed to one William Wolsey. He sold it to John Madden in 1812, and so on, so forth and so frustrating for the respectable middle-class citizenry of the area who loathed the invasion of drunken riff-raff to their genteel suburb for two weeks every summer.

Eventually in 1855 the Committee for the Abolition of Donnybrook Fair raised enough cash, the princely sum of three thousand pounds – or about a quarter of a million euro today – to buy the licence from the Madden family and consign it to perdition.

One lingering memory of the event is the ballad 'The Humours of Donnybrook Fair' sung by, among others, the great Tommy Makem. It includes the lines:

> *To Donnybrook steer, all you sons of Parnassus*
> *Poor painters, poor poets, poor newsmen, poor knaves*
> *To see what the fun is that all fun surpasses*
> *The sorrow and sadness of Erin's green slaves*
> *O Donnybrook, jewel, full of mirth is your quiver*
> *Where all flock from Dublin to gape and to stare*
> *At two elegant bridges, without e'er a river*
> *So success to the humours of Donnybrook Fair.*

The reference in line seven is a tad unreasonable as the Dodder river does flow through the area.

Donnybrook Fair, scene of many scandalous and enervating sights, happy hunting ground of the con artist and the bootlegger, was finally and formally abolished, one hundred and fifty years ago, on this day.

Broadcast 21 August 2015

1 August 1915
Jeremiah O'Donovan Rossa is
Buried in Glasnevin Cemetery

It might well be said of Jeremiah O'Donovan Rossa, that 'nothing became his life like the leaving of it'. He would have been delighted to know that his interment in Glasnevin cemetery in 1915 launched the brief but remarkable career of another Irish revolutionary.

More about that later. Let's first rewind to 1831, the year of Rossa's birth in Rosscarbery, Co. Cork. Twenty-five years later he founded the Phoenix National and Literary Society. It may sound innocuous enough, but its guiding principle was less about reading interesting books and more about the liberation of Ireland by force of arms. No messing about with elections or parliaments for O'Donovan Rossa. His society would later affiliate with the Irish Republican Brotherhood and Rossa's career as a revolutionary nationalist would properly begin.

Two years before the abortive Fenian rising of 1867, Rossa and a number of his colleagues who worked on the organisation's newspaper, the *Irish People*, were arrested and jailed. He was released in 1870 as part of a general amnesty. In his case, however, he had to agree, along with John Devoy, to emigrate to the USA and never come back.

O'Donovan Rossa was no less of a nuisance to the British government in America. Residing in New York he founded a newspaper, the *United Irishman*. This was largely subscription-based with subscribers – whom Rossa called his 'tenants' – paying what the editor described as a weekly 'rent' for the privilege and pleasure of reading his politically extreme outpourings. These went as far as advocating the murder of Irish landlords and even the likes of Prime Minister William Gladstone. Rossa also raised money, via what he called his 'Skirmishing Fund', to finance a bombing campaign in England. This was successfully launched in the early 1880s and caused much destruction, particularly in London. There was even one dynamite attack on the House of Commons. On many occasions the British government sought his extradition but his activities were seen as political actions rather than crimes by the US government. Had he been bombing Washington they might have seen things a bit differently. In 1885 he was shot and wounded by an Englishwoman, Iseult Dudley. The British government claimed that she had not been working for them. Well they would, wouldn't they?

Rossa died in June 1915 at the age of eighty-three. He had actually returned twice to Ireland, in 1894 and 1904, astonishingly, with the approval of the British government. But his *post mortem* return in 1915 was possibly his finest hour. The IRB, at the instigation of the old Fenian Tom Clarke, conscious of the potential propaganda value of a big nationalist funeral, asked Devoy to ship Rossa's body back to Ireland.

After his cortege trailed through the crowded streets of Dublin – Dubliners always loved a big funeral – he was buried in Glasnevin Cemetery. As his coffin was being lowered into the ground, Pádraig Pearse, a relatively unknown figure at the time, stepped out of the crowd and spoke over the grave. He warned the British government that:

> *They think that they have foreseen everything, think that they have provided against everything; but, the fools, the fools, the*

fools! — They have left us our Fenian dead, and while Ireland holds these graves, Ireland unfree shall never be at peace.

Had Rossa been in a position to do so he would have given a loud war whoop in response. Patrick Pearse's short oration, though utterly different in tone, has acquired something of the status of an Irish Gettysburg address. Jeremiah O'Donovan Rossa was buried in Glasnevin Cemetery ninety-nine years ago, on this day.

Broadcast 1 August 2014

7 August 1916
The Premiere of Irish-Produced Film
O'Neil of the Glen

In August 1916 the Battle of the Somme was still raging and thousands of young Irishmen were soon to die in the ruins of the French villages of Guillemont and Ginchy. Thousands of their compatriots were mouldering in British jails and prison camps like Frongoch after participating in the Easter Rising; others were being rounded up as one of the 'usual suspects', even if they had nothing to do with it.

But there was still room for some good old-fashioned entertainment, and one of the more interesting phenomena of the leisure industry in Ireland during World War One was the encroachment of the moving picture on a scene previously dominated by the music hall and popular theatre. It was the beginnings of the triumph of the early cinema and it was only a matter of time before an indigenous Irish film industry sprang up to provide alternatives to the fare provided by US filmmakers which was, increasingly, coming from the American West Coast.

In 1910 the New York based Kalem Film company became the first American outfit to shoot outside the USA when they came to Ireland and filmed the one-reel *A Lad From Old Ireland*, with Sidney Olcott directing.

But in 1916 the Irish lunatics took over the asylum when the Film Company of Ireland was formed by Henry Fitzgibbon and

195

Irish-American James Mark Sullivan. Sullivan had been impressed by D. W. Griffith's epic, *Birth of a Nation,* and felt that something similar, but hopefully far less racist, could be achieved in Ireland.

As a committed Irish nationalist with a desire to make films sympathetic to that cause, Sullivan, to his intense chagrin, was forced to experience the destruction of all his early films in an abortive nationalist uprising. The offices of the Film Company of Ireland were in Sackville Street and were destroyed in the assault on the GPO by the Crown forces. To add insult to injury, Sullivan was himself rounded up as a suspected participant in the Easter Rising, taken to Dublin Castle for questioning and transferred briefly to Kilmainham Jail. He was released on 6 May, so would have been in Kilmainham while the first executions of the 1916 leaders were taking place.

Not to be deterred by the loss of his back catalogue, Sullivan enlisted the aid of some freelance and Abbey Theatre actors and began work on *O'Neil of the Glen.* In this three-reel silent melodrama of about thirty minutes, J. M. Kerrigan directed a cast that included Fred O'Donovan, already famous for his portrayal of Christy Mahon in J. M. Synge's controversial *Playboy of the Western World.*

The film was marketed as the 'first picture play produced by an Irish company with Irish actors in Ireland' so as to leave little doubt about its place of origin. The Unionist *Dublin Evening Mail* praised the film as 'one of the finest cinematographic productions shown for quite some time'. It received an 'A' certificate in Britain, meaning that it could only be seen by 'adults or children accompanied by responsible adults' – the term 'responsible adult' was not defined.

At the premiere, Sullivan did a very clever thing. He filmed the audience enjoying the first night and cut the footage into some of his later movies. This had the 'local newspaper effect' in that people bought tickets for his subsequent films on the basis that they might, at some point, see themselves on the screen.

The Film Company of Ireland went on to make a number of other silents, the most famous being their 1918 feature *Knocknagow*, based on the epic Charles Kickham novel. This starred, and was directed by, Fred O'Donovan. The following year, under cover of shooting an adaptation of Boucicault's *Willy O'Reilly and his Colleen Bawn*, they shot a film seeking funds for the Republican cause. Its distribution methods were unique in film history. As it clearly could not be legally exhibited during the War of Independence, IRA volunteers would simply arrive at cinemas around the country and, at gunpoint, order the projectionist to substitute the Republican Loan film for whatever was being shown. There is more than one way of reaching your audience.

The Film Company of Ireland's *O'Neil of the Glen* received its world premiere at Dublin's Bohemian Theatre, ninety-nine years ago, on this day.

Broadcast 7 August 2015

22 August 1922
Michael Collins is Killed in an
Ambush at Béal na mBláth in Cork

As Eamon de Valera was to discover, a long life and a successful political career do not make for the stuff of legend and romance. Being cut off in your prime, on the other hand, and making a handsome corpse in military uniform, adds yards to the length of your legend. While de Valera achieved a tremendous amount in his life, he simply does not have the allure of the man who became his most famous adversary, Michael Collins.

Collins as a young man was a member of the Irish Republican Brotherhood and a foot soldier in the 1916 Rising. Collins was a willing participant but was determined that no similarly doomed challenge to British power would happen under his watch. When the Crown forces were engaged again, it would be on his terms.

During the three year Anglo-Irish war, Collins was Minister for Finance in the Provisional government. Crucially and famously, however, he was also Director of Intelligence for the IRA. It was in this capacity that he turned the tables on a Dublin Castle accustomed to being able to debilitate revolutionary movements by the use of well-placed informers within their ranks. Collins managed to secure the services of a number of well-placed policemen, men like David Nelligan and Ned Broy, as double-agents who kept him abreast of what was going on in the Dublin Metropolitan Police and Dublin Castle. Collins also, notoriously, gathered together a group of assassins, known simply as The Squad, to exploit the information coming from inside the Castle by eliminating over-enthusiastic policemen, British agents and civil servants.

Collins was noted also for the considerable *élan* with which he travelled through the city of Dublin, despite being Public Enemy Number One. He almost seemed to court detection – there was a reward of ten thousand pounds on his head that was never claimed – by cycling and walking all over the city, often with minimal attempt at disguise.

As with other iconic Irish political leaders, there is much rumour and speculation surrounding his sexual activities. These are referred to in some quarters as 'alleged scandals'. Can the sex life of an unmarried red-blooded twenty-something, who actually had precious little time for liaisons with women, possibly be in any way scandalous? Whatever the truth about his exploits, there is no doubt about his romantic attachment to Kitty Kiernan, with whom he exchanged hundreds of letters.

After the conclusion of the Anglo-Irish Treaty in December 1921, Collins's remark to Lord Birkenhead, the Lord Chancellor, was uncannily prophetic. Birkenhead had observed to the reluctant leader of the Irish delegation that 'I may have signed my political death warrant', to which Collins replied, 'I may have signed my actual death warrant'. In the subsequent Treaty debates he memorably described the document as 'the freedom to achieve freedom'.

There have been four books devoted just to the circumstances of the death of Collins, so it is clearly still a controversial topic. He was advised against making a trip to his native Cork towards the end of the Civil War in 1922. The county was one of the last strongholds of the Republican forces ranged against the infant Irish Free State. Conspiracy theories abound as to how Collins and his guards found themselves involved in an ambush at Béal na mBláth and why he was the only casualty of the encounter.

Michael Collins, just thirty-one years old at the time, died, ninety-two years ago, on this day.

Broadcast 22 August 2014

September

"...to give truth in the news"

12 September 1827
The Birth of Cornelius O'Keefe, Irish Cattleman in Montana

For many nineteenth-century Irishmen and women, deportation to Australia meant permanent residency in that burgeoning colony after their period of detention had expired. Few ever came back to Ireland.

A number of them, however, didn't even complete their term of exile. The famous *Catalpa* rescue was organised in New York by, among others, John Devoy. Among the six Fenian prisoners who got away on that occasion was the famous Irish-American journalist John Boyle O'Reilly.

Corkman Cornelius O'Keefe was transported to Van Diemen's Land, now Tasmania, in the early 1850s for his political activities. These would have been similar to those of Devoy and O'Reilly. He too managed to make his escape from captivity, hitch a lift on a boat and make it to New York by 1853.

Realising that the American West provided more opportunity to the newly arrived Irishman than the highly stratified society of the East Coast, he shipped for California via Cape Horn in the late 1850s. After a short period as a labourer he settled in Montana and became a highly progressive rancher. He farmed on irrigated land and imported the first threshing machine, reaper and mower into the territory of Montana. As he built up his land-holding he also survived many attacks from native American tribes who were gradually being dispossessed of their lands by the Federal authorities and moved onto reservations.

A large man with a violent temper (he once wrecked a court after disagreeing with a judge's verdict), he acquired the nickname 'The Baron' and never quite shook off his Irish disrespect for authority. In the early 1860s a well-organised gang known (to themselves), as 'The Innocents', was terrorising Montana mining towns. The gang was led by Henry Plummer who – this was the 'Wild West' after all – also happened to be town sheriff of the small settlement of Bannack, Montana. This is now a ghost town in Beaverhead County. The Innocents were to Montana what the infamous Hole in the Wall gang, led by Butch Cassidy, Henry Longabaugh (aka the Sundance Kid) and Kid Curry, was to nearby Wyoming.

As was the custom in the West, an equally well-organised group of vigilantes began to make inroads into the Innocents' activities and lynched many members of the gang. One of the most notorious Innocent gangsters, Robert Zachary, in his flight from the vigilantes, sought and was granted temporary refuge on O'Keefe's ranch. When Zachary's pursuers caught up with him, O'Keefe – with typical Irish hospitality – refused to hand him over until he had given him breakfast. He argued to the members of the vigilance committee that 'you can't hang a man on an empty stomach'. Zachary was duly fed, tried informally and hanged expeditiously. (For the record, Plummer was later betrayed by one of his former henchmen and himself hanged.)

O'Keefe's act of civil disobedience didn't greatly damage his reputation in Montana. He became Missoula County Commissioner in 1872 and also served in the Montana state legislature. He died of Bright's disease in 1883.

Irish nationalist, transportee, escapee, and Montana cattleman and politician Cornelius O'Keefe, was born in Cork, one hundred and eighty-seven years ago, on this day.

Broadcast 12 September 2014

11 September 1838
The Birth of Irish-American Prelate
John Ireland

The American Roman Catholic Church can be a very conservative institution indeed, and few Irish-American prelates have a reputation for being on the progressive wing of that conservative institution. That's why John Ireland, Kilkenny-born bishop of the Twin Cities of St Paul/Minnesota, stands out. He was a nineteenth-century political progressive on issues like Church/State relations, education and immigration. He was friendly with two American Presidents, Theodore Roosevelt and William McKinley, and was vocally opposed to the widespread political corruption of the late nineteenth century USA and to racial inequality. Cardinal Paul Cullen he was not.

So it's something of a shame that, in Minnesota at least, he is best-remembered, none too fondly by some, for his encounter with a group of fishermen from Connemara in the 1880s.

Ireland, disturbed by reports of the economic conditions being experienced by Irish immigrants in eastern American cities, and conscious of the need to populate the wide-open spaces of the Minnesota hinterland, established colonies with names like Clontarf, Avoca and Iona, that provided land and a fresh start for impoverished Irish-American urban dwellers. The Kilkenny-born Archbishop was highly successful in populating the often inhospitable prairies with pockets of Irish settlements through his Catholic Colonisation Bureau. The project brought more than four thousand families from eastern slums onto four hundred thousand acres of farmland in rural Minnesota. Many of the colonies remain relatively intact to this day.

Ireland's right-hand man in this enterprise was Roscommon man Dillon O'Brien, born into the Catholic landholding class, who had been financially ruined by the Famine and forced to emigrate.

However, the philanthropic Archbishop had an unhappy experience when he agreed to take on a group of impoverished fisherman from the West of Ireland whom he misguidedly attempted to turn into frontier farmers. The saga of the 'Connemaras' is part of the lore of the American Midwest.

Ireland had to be coaxed into accepting the fishermen and their families in the first place. He allowed himself to be persuaded to take them on but the wisdom of his initial reluctance was rapidly justified. The fifty or so families that came from Connemara were coastal inhabitants. When Dillon O'Brien's son first saw them he was not impressed. He described the group, mostly monoglot Irish speakers, as 'not the competent, but the incompetent; not the industrious, but the shiftless; a group composed of mendicants who knew nothing about farming'.

They were settled near a pre-existing colony called Graceville. The settlers already there were even less well-disposed towards their new neighbours than O'Brien's son. The timing of their arrival was unfortunate as well. It coincided with the harsh prairie winter. Opportunities for planting were not promising as the soil was only to be penetrated with pickaxes rather than ploughs or spades. One of the first things the bewildered fisher-folk did was eat or sell the seed crops allocated to them.

Ireland was forced to find employment for many members of the group in Minneapolis and St Paul. Worse still, from his point of view, was the charitable intervention of the local Freemasons. The 'Connemaras', happy to accept assistance from any source, had no awareness of the antagonism that existed between the overwhelmingly Protestant Masons and the American Roman Catholic Church. Ireland spoke out against the donors and the recipients. As few of the 'Connemaras' had any English, their right of reply was somewhat circumscribed. In attacking such obvious underdogs for accepting the charity of members of a highly respected organisation, Ireland lost some of his progressive gloss.

Today a street that runs from the Cathedral of St Paul to the Minnesota State Capitol building is named after him. Despite his brush with the 'Connemaras', he is still held in high regard.

John Ireland, Catholic Archbishop of the Twin Cities, was born, one hundred and seventy-seven years ago, on this day.

Broadcast 11 September 2015

4 September 1844
The House of Lords Frees
Daniel O'Connell from Prison

1843 was to have been Repeal Year. A series of huge gatherings, dubbed 'monster meetings' by the hostile *Times* of London, was designed to put pressure on the British government to restore an Irish parliament.

Of course, it didn't happen, and an almost inevitable consequence of the failure of the Repeal movement was the arrest and prosecution in 1844 of its leaders, the principal motive force being Daniel O'Connell, the architect of Catholic Emancipation.

The charge against the Liberator and a small number of key allies, including his son John, was one of conspiracy. As defined in the mid nineteenth century, this tended to reverse what we would see as the natural order of justice. Essentially, the accused had to prove that they were *not* involved in a conspiracy rather than the onus falling on the Crown to prove that they were.

The fact that, in essence, many potential Catholic jurors were excluded from the jury panel, didn't help O'Connell's cause. There were four presiding judges, led by Chief Justice Pennefather, a man described by one of the defendants, the *Nation* newspaper editor Charles Gavan Duffy, as 'descended from a family of Puritan[s] … gorged with lands and offices during the penal times, but still on the watch for ministerial favours ….' So no help to be expected from that quarter.

The defence case was also placed at a severe disadvantage by the refusal of the Crown to supply them with even a list of witnesses. Try that today and see how far you get. Evidence was introduced by the prosecution from official government note-takers of the allegedly seditious speeches made by O'Connell and others at the 'monster' meetings.

The almost inevitable result of the lengthy trial was the conviction of the accused, helped by a summing up from the Chief Justice that read like a continuation of the closing address of the prosecution. Anything Pennefather felt the Attorney General had left out, he generously supplied himself.

So, at the advanced age of sixty-nine and in bad health, O'Connell became a felon. But his punishment was in inverse proportion to the supposed gravity of the crime. O'Connell and his fellow prisoners were allowed to choose their own place of incarceration. They opted for the Richmond Bridewell, a prison mainly used to accommodate debtors, on Dublin's South Circular Road.

O'Connell and his fellow inmates actually served out their sentences in the comfort of the homes of the Governor and Deputy Governor rather than in prison cells. In time, the entire episode would become known as 'the Richmond picnic'. Hailed as a martyr for the nationalist cause, O'Connell's Richmond experience was, in truth, 'martyrdom deluxe'. One of the detainees wrote that 'the imprisonment proved as little unpleasant as a holiday in a country house'.

Not only were the prisoners afforded the facility of having their spouses present at all times – O'Connell did not avail of this as he was a widower – they were also allowed their own servants. Food was imported from eating-houses outside the walls of the prison or, more often than not, provided by hundreds of well-wishers. O'Connell, enabled to take daily exercise, regained much of his health.

The main source of irritation was the huge number of visitors anxious to meet with O'Connell as he was no longer a moving target. That was quickly sorted by a ban on visitors, imposed by the privileged inmates, outside of a four-hour window from noon to 4.00 p.m.

One aspect of the incarceration in which the Irish public were not permitted to share was O'Connell's growing infatuation with a woman young enough to be his granddaughter, Rose McDowell, daughter of a Belfast Presbyterian merchant. He corresponded with her and may even have proposed to her. To the relief of his family, she was not interested in becoming the second Mrs O'Connell.

The Liberator, despite the massive celebration that marked his release, may well have had mixed feelings when the House of Lords reversed his conviction, one hundred and seventy-one years ago, on this day.

Broadcast 4 September 2015

19 September 1845
The Birth of Thomas Barnardo, Irish Humanitarian

His name is probably more celebrated today than it was at the time of his death at the age of sixty in 1905. What is probably not as well-known is that Thomas Barnardo, whose charities have rescued and housed hundreds of thousands of destitute or endangered children since 1870, was a Dubliner.

He was born just as the Great Famine began to grip the country of his birth. This may or may not have had some influence on his future career as a notable philanthropist. Of equal importance may well have been the fact that he had sixteen siblings. His father was a furrier who left Hamburg in Germany and came to Dublin in the middle of the nineteenth century. He married twice and fathered seventeen children.

Barnardo himself was educated at St Patrick's Cathedral School and left Dublin in 1866 to study medicine in London, where he became a fellow of the Royal College of Surgeons. While there he also performed much charitable and evangelical work for the city's poor. He thus became aware of the number of vulnerable children in the city – the numbers had hardly declined since the publication of Charles Dickens's *Oliver Twist* in the 1830s. London was still coping with the effects of the industrial revolution and a population explosion that made areas like the East End of the city a byword for bad housing, inadequate hygiene and rampant disease. For example, a few months after Barnardo's arrival in the city, an outbreak of cholera killed more than three thousand people in the East End.

His intention had been to pursue a career as a medical missionary in China. Instead, he remained in London and founded his first children's home – for boys – in Stepney in 1870. Over the door was the sign 'No destitute child ever refused admission'. His wife, Syrie, had received a sixty acre landholding as a wedding gift, and the couple turned that into a rural retreat for impoverished and vulnerable London girls. By the time of his death, thirty-five years after he began his great work, Barnardo had established more than one hundred homes around the UK and had housed more than sixty thousand endangered and/or impoverished children. Many had been sleeping rough on the streets, others had been rescued from factory work and other inappropriate forms of employment.

One of Barnardo's own five children, named Syrie after her mother, went on to become a leading interior decorator. She was married twice, first to Henry Wellcome, owner of the pharmaceutical giant. After their divorce in 1917 she married the writer Somerset Maugham. They divorced in 1928.

At the time of his death in 1905, Barnardo homes were catering for almost ten thousand children annually. In 1989 the organisation founded a section in his native Ireland. It now operates forty branches in local communities across the country.

Dr Thomas Barnardo, internationally renowned philanthropist, was born in Dame Street in Dublin, one hundred and sixty-nine years ago, on this day.

Broadcast 19 September 2014

18 September 1867
Thomas Kelly and Timothy Deasy
Freed by Fenians in Manchester

No one paid too much attention to the new MP for County Meath, returned in an 1875 by-election to a House of Commons dominated by Disraeli's Tories. He was left entirely to his own devices until June 1876 when the Chief Secretary for Ireland, Sir Michael Hicks Beach, was addressing the House and made reference to 'the Manchester murderers'. The Honourable Member for Meath was quickly on his feet and angrily informed the Tory Chief Secretary that he did not 'believe, and never shall believe, that any murder was committed at Manchester'. Thus was the world alerted to the political philosophy of Charles Stewart Parnell.

But what was the Manchester reference all about? Who were the so-called 'murderers' being condemned by Hicks Beach?

The story probably begins with an Irish-American from Mountbellew in Co. Galway, Thomas Kelly, and his service on the Union side in the American Civil War. Kelly, the son of a farmer and publican, had been educated at St Jarlath's College in Tuam. There he came under the particular influence of one of his teachers, nationalist activist Michael Joseph MacCann, composer of the song 'O'Donnell Abu', familiar to RTÉ Radio listeners in the days when the station used to go off the air for a few hours each night.

Kelly emigrated to New York at the age of eighteen but took his Republican ideals along with him. He distinguished himself in the American Civil War and, subsequently, like many Irish-American veterans, joined the newly formed Fenian Brotherhood. He was instrumental in first collaborating with, and then deposing, the vacillating IRB leader, James Stephens. Ironically, one of his first acts as the putative Head Centre of the IRB was to help spring Stephens from Richmond Jail in December 1866. He also planned the abortive Fenian raid on Chester Castle in England in February 1867. Not the IRB's finest hour.

After the debacle that was the 1867 Fenian rising, Kelly was arrested, escaped from prison and was then recaptured in Manchester after being brought in along with a Fenian associate, Timothy Deasy, for loitering. Kelly and Deasy gave the police assumed names, calling themselves Martin Williams and John Whyte, but they were soon recognised and sent for trial.

They were being transferred between courthouse and jail in Manchester on 18 September 1867 when a crowd of around thirty Fenians surrounded their prison van in an attempt to free them. A shot was fired at the lock of the door at the rear of the vehicle. It failed to achieve its purpose but instead killed a policeman, Sergeant Charles Brett, who was guarding the prisoners. Another prisoner travelling in the van took the keys from Brett's body and handed them through the grille to the would-be rescuers. Kelly and Deasy managed to escape completely in the confusion that followed but a number of their liberators were later arrested and charged with murder.

Five of them were convicted and three, William Philip Allen, Michael Larkin and Michael O'Brien, were publicly hanged at Salford jail on 23 November 1867. It was these three men, dubbed the Manchester Martyrs in Irish Republican mythology, that Michael Hicks Beach called the 'Manchester Murderers' before he was rudely interrupted by the previously anonymous Honourable Member for County Meath.

Kelly and Deasy, whose freedom had been bought at huge cost: the lives of four men, were never recaptured and managed to make it to the USA. Kelly later secured a good job as a US Customs official. He lived on until 1908.

The successful but ultimately counter-productive attempt to free Thomas Kelly and Timothy Deasy from police custody in Manchester took place, one hundred and forty-eight years ago, on this day.

Broadcast 18 September 2015

25 September 1880
The Murder of Galway Landlord, Lord Mountmorres

It would probably be safe to say that for every week Ireland spent in the throes of rebellion in the course of our history, we spent a year involved in serious and often violent land agitation.

The 1830s and 1880s in particular were times of agrarian uproar as the Tithe War, the Land War and the Plan of Campaign dominated the political and social agendas. From the Land War came the word and the practice of 'boycotting' – a peaceful but effective form of isolation of despised and uncooperative landlords. But sometimes the tactics employed on both sides were less than peaceful and distinctly unpalatable. The term 'Ribbonism' was used to describe the activities of the members of illegal secret societies who took direct action against those opposed to the interests of the tenants. The term Royal Irish Constabulary was used to describe the response of the authorities.

One of the myths of the periods of agrarian violence that frequently bedevilled rural Ireland was that members of Ribbon societies spent their evenings running around with blackened faces killing landlords. Nothing could be further from the truth. Not that many Ribbonmen would have objected to doing violence to their friendly neighbourhood aristocrats, it was just that they rarely got close enough to take a pot shot at them. More at risk were the agents of the landlords, bailiffs who did their bidding, fellow tenants who did something inadvisable – like taking on land vacated by someone who had been evicted, aka 'land grabbers' – or, more often than not, completely innocent livestock.

One significant exception, however, was an extremely modest landlord based in Clonbur in Co. Galway: Lord Mountmorres. He was 'modest' in the context of the size of his holdings. He was one of the smallest landlords in the country with only eleven tenants producing an annual income of around three hundred pounds. The country's bigger landlords – there were about ten thousand landed families altogether – would have boasted twenty thousand or more acres, and incomes of more than ten thousand pounds a year. Unlike some of his peers, Mountmorres was not known for evicting his tenants, led a relatively frugal lifestyle in the unpretentious Ebor House and was said to be quite popular in the part of Galway where he lived. So why was he shot dead a few miles from his home in September 1880 when another Galway landlord, the loathsome and avaricious Lord Clanricarde, notorious for evicting tenants, avoided a similar fate?

Two reasons come to mind. Firstly, Clanricarde didn't regularly take to the roads of Galway in a horse and trap – he spent his life in London and paid others to do his dirty work. Secondly, when you scratch the surface of the 'benign landlord' narrative that surrounds Mountmorres, you find someone who was not nearly as popular as he was cracked up to be.

Mountmorres was shot at around 8.00 p.m. on the evening of 25 September. He was driving alone between Clonbur and Ebor House. When his horse and carriage made it home without their driver the alarm was raised. His body was quickly found. He had been shot six times, some of the shots were at close range, and he had obviously died quickly at the scene. A local family, the Flanagans, refused to allow the corpse to be taken into their house before it was finally removed, saying that 'if they admitted it, nothing belonging to [them] would be alive this day twelve months'.

Despite a one thousand pound reward being offered for information, no one came forward. One of Mountmorres's tenants, Patrick Sweeney, who had been served with an eviction notice, was suspected, but no one was ever convicted, or even tried for the murder.

Later on, Michael Davitt would claim that Mountmorres had been killed because he 'eked out his wretched income as a landlord by doing spy's work for the Castle'. When Lady Mountmorres testified at a tribunal investigating agrarian crime in the late 1880s she claimed that the atmosphere had changed in the locality after Sweeney was issued with his eviction order: 'The men ceased to touch their hats, and they were disrespectful in their manner'. She later fainted under cross-examination.

It emerged that Mountmorres had little time for the activities of the newly formed Land League, had sought police protection and demanded that the army be brought into the area to suppress the activities of the League. None of this was calculated to increase his popularity.

But, the truth is that we will never know who killed Viscount Mountmorres, and precisely why he was murdered, one hundred and thirty-five years ago, on this day.

Broadcast 25 September 2015

26 September 1904
The Death of Hiberno-Japanese Writer Lafcadio Hearn

Though he could have claimed to be Greek and although the Japanese themselves might claim him and his writings, Patrick Lafcadio Hearn is indisputably Irish, although far better known in the Orient than he is here. Let's face it, there aren't many Irish authors who wrote under the pen name Koizumi Yakumo.

His middle name, Lafcadio, comes from the Greek island of his birth, Lefkada, where the great lyric poet Sappho is supposed to have committed suicide. He was the son of a British army surgeon stationed on the island in 1850, the year Hearn was born there. But at the age of two his mother took him to Dublin and he spent his formative years in the suburb of Rathmines and his boyhood summers in Tramore, Co. Waterford. His Greek mother had some trouble adapting to Irish life – and presumably the Irish climate. Hearn's childhood was not enhanced by the suspicion of his extended family that he had been born out of wedlock and that his father and mother were not actually married. This was because his extended family was Protestant and did not hold with a marriage that had taken place in the Greek Orthodox Church.

At the age of nineteen Hearn said goodbye to Ireland and went to live in the USA. There he made a living as a journalist, first in Cincinnati and then in the party town of New Orleans. Prior to leaving Ohio, Hearn had already acquired a reputation as a crime reporter, and became renowned for his coverage of a number of lurid murders. He also married an African-American woman, Mattie Foley; inter-racial marriage was still illegal at the time, 1875, a decade after the end of the Civil War, even in Northern states. They divorced in 1877.

Hearn spent a decade in New Orleans, immersing himself in Creole culture and writing about the French and Caribbean roots of the Louisiana city. He has had more books written about him than any other former New Orleans resident, apart from Louis Armstrong – though they have not proved particularly popular in the Big Easy as they are mostly in Japanese. His former home in the city, on Cleveland Avenue, has been preserved as an historical monument.

From New Orleans Hearn, now in his forties, travelled to Japan in 1890. He settled at first in Matsue in western Japan and married Koizumi Setsu, the daughter of an old noble samurai family. Between 1894 and his death in 1905 he produced more than fifteen volumes of stories, poems, and non-fiction writings on his adopted country. He was one of the main foreign interpreters of the country as it began to open up to the outside world – and conquer parts of it. A volume of Hearn's ghost stories, *Kwaidan*, was turned into a movie by the Japanese director Masaki Kobayashi in 2007.

Hearn may not be as well known in his native Ireland as he is in Japan, but the creator of James Bond, Ian Fleming, had certainly heard of him. In his 1964 novel *You Only Live Twice* Fleming has the villain Blofeld ask Bond if he is familiar with the Japanese phrase *kirisute gomen*. Bond, lip-curlingly responds, 'Spare me the Lafcadio Hearn, Blofeld'. For the record, *kirisute gomen* is what allowed samurai to kill any member of the lower orders without compunction if they looked sideways at them.

In March of this year it was announced that the Japanese government was to contribute to the construction of a Japanese garden in honour of the writer in Tramore.

Patrick Lafcadio Hearn, well-travelled writer, died one hundred and ten years ago, on this day.

Broadcast 26 September 2014

5 September 1931
The First Edition of the *Irish Press*
Rolls Off the Presses

It's often said that only a supreme optimist sets up a business in the middle of a depression. That means that Eamon de Valera must either have felt it was his lucky day or figured that he needed a newspaper supportive of his political party when he established the *Irish Press* in September 1931. It was two years after the Wall Street Crash and at the beginning of, as it transpired, the Great Depression.

The *Irish Press* had officially been registered three years before, two years after de Valera had chosen to end his boycott of Dáil Éireann, had split his remnant of the original Sinn Féin, and had created Fianna Fáil. Dev's avowed aim in creating his own newspaper was 'to give the truth in the news', the implication being that *Independent* newspapers and the *Irish Times* were somewhat unfamiliar with the concept.

The money used to establish the *Press* had an interesting history. It had been raised by de Valera during his fractious visit to the USA in 1920 to raise funds for the War of Independence. Instead of being handed over to the Minister for Finance, Michael Collins, the five million or so collected was left in banks in New York, and ultimately found its way into the start-up funds of the newspaper.

The presses for the first issue of the new paper were, ceremonially, set rolling by Margaret Pearse, mother of Patrick and

Willie Pearse. The front page was almost entirely devoted to the serious flooding that was inundating the country. *Plus ça change, plus c'est la même chose.* The orientation of the *Irish Press*, as opposed to, say, the *Irish Times*, can be gleaned from its first off-lead, with the headline informing readers: 'Convents thrown open to succour homeless'. De Valera and the future Fianna Fáil leader, Jack Lynch, were always keen on securing the convent vote in general elections.

In the bottom right hand-corner of page one there is an advertisement for Pierce Farm Machinery that seems more appropriate to the 1830s than the 1930s, depression or no depression. It might well have appealed to De Valera's Spartan and ascetic sensibilities. It shows a farmer hand-ploughing a field behind two substantial horses. A murder of crows hovers overhead. A smaller drawing depicts what looks like an African farmer of some ill-defined period of pre-history hand-ploughing behind a single oxen. The advertisement is dominated by the word 'Progress' in large, bold print. However, the only indication of progress appears to be the domestication of the horse and the fact that the 'modern' farmer has two animals with which to share his burden rather than one.

The *Irish Press* was quickly in trouble. Its first editor, Frank Gallagher, was fined fifty pounds for alleging that the Gardaí had ill-treated anti-Treaty republicans.

Among those who wrote or worked for the paper from 1931, until its closure in 1995, with the loss of six hundred jobs, were Patrick Kavanagh, Tim Pat Coogan, Vincent Browne, Con Houlihan, John O'Shea, Mary Kenny and John Banville.

The first edition of the *Irish Press* was printed, eighty-three years ago, on this day.

Broadcast 5 September 2014

October

"I say old man would you mind? Hand it over"

23 October 1641
The Beginning of the 1641 Rebellion

It was a co-ordinated attempt at a *coup d'état* – designed to use the element of surprise and gain a bloodless victory, but bloodless it certainly wasn't. The 1641 Rebellion has gone down as one of the most horrifying in the long history of Irish rebellions.

The idea was to seize Dublin Castle while taking military action elsewhere around the country. A plan was formulated by the Leinster chieftain Rory O'Moore and executed by the Ulster warlord Phelim O'Neill. It just didn't work. The rebels failed to take the Castle because their plan had been betrayed to the authorities by one of the many informers in that same long history of Irish rebellion, in this instance one Owen O'Connolly, a Catholic convert to Protestantism.

Why did the Catholic Irish stage a rebellion in 1641? As usual there was a multitude of reasons, including political, social, economic and cultural.

The political situation in England, where King Charles I was at loggerheads with his parliament and the Scots over issues of religion and sovereignty, impacted on Ireland as well. Scotland was defying the monarchy and the English parliament was refusing to grant money to the King to raise an army to put down the stroppy northerners. A proposal to raise an Irish Catholic army to put manners on Scotland instead gave rise to anxiety in England, as well as to suggestions that it was time the English put manners on the uppity Irish again.

Allied to that was resentment on the part of those dispossessed in the plantations of the sixteenth and seventeenth centuries. Many Irish Catholic landowners had been displaced by English Protestants. They, not unnaturally, wanted their lands returned, by fair means or foul. Many also wanted their language and religion back – rebels in Co. Cavan, for example, rose, as they put it, in the name of religion and banned the use of the English language in the county.

Even the Little Ice Age played a part. This period of global cooling was especially severe in the seventeenth century and had an impact on Irish harvests. Irish Catholic grandees who had actually managed to retain their lands were on the verge of bankruptcy. With interest rates as high as thirty per cent, many were in a state worse than debt. Phelim O'Neill and Rory O'Moore were amongst those who were liable to lose their lands to their creditors.

Failure to take Dublin Castle was counteracted to some extent by success across Ulster, the scene of the most successful and disruptive plantation in the early 1600s. That initial success, however, led to one of the most distressing and counter-productive pogroms ever unleashed in this country as settlers were violently dispossessed by the prior owners of their lands. The 1641 massacres in Ulster, recounted *ex post facto* and recorded in hundreds of depositions now stored in Trinity College, Dublin, were predictable and horrendous, and were used to justify the subsequent merciless revenge of Cromwell's forces in Ireland and an Ulster Protestant siege mentality.

No one knows exactly how many Ulster Protestants were slaughtered in 1641. English Cromwellian propagandists came up with the ludicrous but provocative figure of two hundred thousand. In the mid seventeenth century that figure would have been greater than the entire Protestant population of Ulster. More considered estimates put direct killings at around four thousand with a total of ten to twelve thousand deaths attributable to murder, disease and hypothermia. The actual figures are probably less important than the profound psychological impact of the slaughter in places like Portadown. There, more than one hundred Protestants were forced into the River Bann where they drowned, were shot or died of exposure. This was, in part at least, in retaliation for the massacre of Catholics by settlers after the defeat of the rebel forces at Lisnagarvey in Co. Antrim.

In 1662 the Irish parliament decreed that 23 October was to be observed as a day of thanksgiving for the deliverance of Protestant Ulster from the hands of their murderous Catholic neighbours. Annual church services would remind Protestants of the 1641 massacres for another century and more.

The 1641 Rebellion, in which the status of non-combatant appears not to have existed, began three hundred and seventy-four years ago, on this day.

Broadcast 23 October 2015

17 October 1738
The Loathsome Aristocrat,
Arthur Rochfort, Fights a Duel

In eighteenth-century Ireland, if you considered yourself to be a gentleman and you were insulted by someone of similar status you didn't a) take it lying down or, b) bring them to court and sue them – you challenged them to a duel and tried to shoot or stab them to death.

One of the more quarrelsome gentlemen of the first half of the 1700s was Arthur Rochfort, a Westmeath grandee whose family had occupied land around Mullingar since the thirteenth century. The town of Rochfortbridge is called after the Rochforts.

Arthur Rochfort was a Justice of the Peace, a man who exercised considerable power over the lesser orders from the bench. In 1737 he was challenged to a duel by one Thomas Nugent. Nugent's beef was that Rochfort had jailed one of his servants for poaching and carrying arms. Proper order really. Nothing came of that particular challenge because the authorities got wind of it and prosecuted Nugent before he could do any damage. They weren't having one of their magistrates shot up by an argumentative aristocrat.

Rochfort, however, did make it into the 'lists' (a form of medieval hand-to-hand combat) the following year when he had another quarrel, this one with an influential member of the Freemasons, Dillon Hampson Pollard. In the shoot-out that followed the challenge, Rochfort came off better, hitting his opponent in the stomach. Fortunately for him, J. P. Pollard recovered. He died of natural causes two years later.

Rochfort's own end was quite ignominious. As it happened he was the proud owner of two irascible, litigious and obnoxious brothers, Robert and George. Robert would go on to become the 1st Earl of Belvedere and build Belvedere House, located outside Mullingar.

Robert had married a beautiful young Dublin heiress, Mary Molesworth. They didn't get on – few people did see eye to eye with the arrogant future Lord Belvedere – but Mary produced three children for him before he became bored with her and arbitrarily accused her of having an affair with Arthur. Arthur denied all carnal knowledge of the alleged relationship. However, either cowed or convinced by friends that an admission of guilt would get her a divorce, Mary admitted adultery. For her supposed sins she was incarcerated for most of the rest of her life in one of the houses on the Belvedere estate while Arthur was forced to flee the country. When he came back, Robert sued him for criminal conversation anyway, won a massive judgment of two thousand pounds and when that was not forthcoming had his brother committed to the Marshalsea Debtors prison in Dublin, where he died. They took their sibling rivalries very seriously in the eighteenth century.

Later on, the charming Robert fell out with his other brother George. The latter had the effrontery to build a bigger and finer mansion within sight of Belvedere House. Robert erected a folly – looking something like a ruined monastery – to cut off his view of George's new manor. It became known, and still is known as, 'the Jealous Wall'. Neither Robert nor George, two utterly disagreeable gentlemen, were ever heard to express any regret at the passing of their brother Arthur.

Incidentally, among the apparent descendants of the Rochforts is a certain former Kerry TD, the late, and extremely agreeable, Jackie Healy Rae.

Arthur Rochfort almost killed Dillon Hampson Pollard in a duel, two hundred and seventy-six years ago, on this day.

Broadcast 17 October 2014

3 October 1750
The Hanging of James McLaine,
Gentleman Highwayman

He's had the privilege of being played on-screen by Johnny Lee Miller, but the bad fortune to have had a losing encounter with the hangman in order to earn that distinction.

The eighteenth-century 'gentleman' James McLaine was born in Monaghan in 1724. His father was from a God-fearing Scottish Presbyterian family. His brother was a churchman. But James was neither God-fearing nor churchy. He was a talented and celebrated eighteenth-century mugger – a toff, but a glorified robber nonetheless.

He was known as 'the gentleman highwayman', though much of his best work was actually done in Hyde Park, which was a lot more lawless in the 1740s than it is today. His accomplice in crime was William Plunkett, an impecunious apothecary – that's a chemist in eighteenth-century language. Both became the anti-heroes of a 1999 movie, *Plunkett and Macleane,* starring Miller and Robert Carlyle as the eponymous outlaws.

McLaine moved from Monaghan to Dublin as a young man and succeeded in spending whatever money he had been given by his father to set up as a merchant. It all went on wine, women and song. Mostly wine and women, actually. Having rapidly worn out his welcome and line of credit in Dublin he made for London and quickly fell into his new line of work with his equally felonious business partner.

The two were known as the 'gentlemen highwaymen' because of the good manners with which they went about the business of taking other people's money and valuables, right down to their often elaborate waistcoats. *Noblesse oblige* was the order of the day when they robbed people like the writer and Whig politician Horace Walpole, son of a prime minister, and Alexander Montgomerie, 10th Earl of Eglinton, a Scottish peer who introduced James Boswell to London.

So anxious was McLaine to preserve the image of fastidiously courteous conduct that when a pistol was discharged in the robbery of Walpole he actually wrote a letter to the owner of the magnificent Strawberry Hill mansion, insisting that it had been an accident and offering to return all the goods stolen for forty pounds.

The money raised in the numerous robberies conducted by the two highwaymen was quickly spent in maintaining the opulent lifestyle to which they became accustomed.

The pair's final robbery, however, turned out to be a waistcoat too far. When McLaine tried to pawn the richly appointed garment stolen from the occupant of a stage coach, it was recognised and the potential purchaser shopped the genteel outlaw to claim the price on his head.

McLaine's trial – he was found guilty without the jury leaving the courtroom – caused something of sensation and he was reported to have been visited by up to three thousand people while awaiting execution. The latter figure is highly unlikely, as is the suggestion that he was the basis for the character of MacHeath in the *Beggar's Opera*. In the latter instance, he would have been only four years of age when John Gay wrote the piece.

For the record, William Plunkett escaped scot free for his part in McLaine's crimes and is reported to have fled to the USA and died there at the age of one hundred.

The Irish-born, London-based highwayman James McLaine was twenty-six years old when he was hanged by the neck until dead, two hundred and sixty-four years ago, on this day.

Broadcast 3 October 2014

30 October 1751
The Birth of Playwright and
Politician Richard Brinsley Sheridan

He was one of the most outstanding English playwrights and politicians of the eighteenth century. However, like many other exceptional exponents of the benign art of theatre and the dark arts of politics, he wasn't English – he was Irish.

Richard Brinsley Sheridan was born in Dorset Street in Dublin in 1751. His surroundings were slightly more fashionable then than they are now. Judging from his parents, he was probably born to write for the theatre. His mother Frances was a playwright and novelist, his father Thomas was, for a long time, an actor-manager.

His budding theatrical and political careers almost failed to get off the ground, however. Sheridan, to defend the honour of his future wife, Elizabeth Linley, was obliged to fight a duel against one Thomas Matthews, a rival for Elizabeth's affections. Matthews who also happened to be married had churlishly defamed Elizabeth in a newspaper article when she rejected his advances.

The two men met twice in 1772. Swords were the weapons of choice on both occasions. At the first encounter, in London, Matthews posed few difficulties for the Irishman. He was quickly disarmed, begged for his life and was forced to retract the defamatory article. Matthews, however, insisted on a rematch and Sheridan decided to oblige him. The second meeting, in Bath, was a much bloodier affair and Sheridan barely survived. According to contemporary accounts he was borne from the field with his opponent's broken sword sticking from his ear and his whole body covered in wounds.

Sheridan survived and three years later produced *The Rivals,* his first play – a sparkling comedy which included the character of a hot-blooded and mean-spirited Irish duellist Sir Lucius O'Trigger. The comedy, coincidentally, is set in Bath. There is more than one way of gaining revenge on a loathsome adversary.

The most memorable character in the play was the sublime Mrs Malaprop, a lady much given to hilarious verbal solecisms. Hence such infamous howlers as her reference to 'an allegory on the banks of the Nile' and 'he can tell you the perpendiculars'. She also refers to another character as 'the very pineapple of politeness'.

His greatest work, which appeared two years later, in 1777, was *The School for Scandal.* Still performed today, it matches and surpasses most of Oscar Wilde's comedies of manners with its acid observations on contemporary social mores and the endless capacity for evil gossip in eighteenth-century London society.

In 1780 Sheridan essentially bribed his way into the House of Commons, as you often did in those days. The franchise in his constituency was fortunately small as each vote cost him a reported five guineas. In Parliament he allied himself to the Whig faction led by Charles James Fox and sided with the American colonials in their disputes with England. In one celebrated and highly theatrical aside in 1793 his fellow Irishman Edmund Burke was ranting about French revolutionary spies and saboteurs. After a rhetorical flourish to emphasise the dangers of allowing Johnny Foreigner access to England, Burke threw a knife onto the floor of the Commons. This drew the retort from Sheridan 'where's the fork?'

Although he was an accomplished parliamentary orator and briefly held political office, one of Sheridan's reasons for retaining his seat in the Commons was probably to evade his creditors. When he lost his seat in 1812 they pounced. He died in poverty three years later, but is buried in Poets Corner in Westminster Abbey.

Sheridan is responsible for many memorable, pithy and witty phrases. He once said of a political opponent that 'the right honourable gentleman is indebted to his memory for his jests and to his imagination for his facts'. In his 1779 play, *The Critic,* he had one of his characters make the very politically apposite observation that 'the number of those who undergo the fatigue of judging for themselves is very small indeed'.

Richard Brinsley Sheridan, playwright, politician and sometime duellist, was born two hundred and sixty-four years ago, on this day.

Broadcast 30 October 2015

10 October 1771
American Emissary Benjamin Franklin Visits the Irish Parliament

There was, understandably, a lot of excitement in Ireland in the summer of 1963 when John F. Kennedy became the first American President to make an official visit to the country. It was a significant moment – the first Irish-American Roman Catholic President was returning to the land his forefathers had left in the 1840s.

But perhaps of more significance, for the USA at least, was a much earlier and much longer visit by a great American luminary almost two centuries before.

Benjamin Franklin was already an eminent scientist and inventor, as well as a printer, publisher and philosopher, before he was despatched by the American colonies to Britain in 1764 to represent their economic and trade interests with the motherland. His mission was not exactly crowned with outstanding success. He was ignored by Lord Hillsborough, Secretary of State for the Colonies, who steadfastly refused to meet him. The British government showed no sign whatever of being prepared to make concessions to their American brethren on the issues of tariffs or taxation. Despite this, Franklin was convinced that they could be persuaded to negotiate and that a more muscular American response would not be necessary.

Until, that is, he visited Ireland in September 1771. At the time, Ireland had its own parliament but its decisions were totally circumscribed by the British administration. Franklin was allowed to visit the entirely Protestant parliament and sit in the House of Commons with the members of that assembly. Afterwards he wrote that 'by joining our interests with theirs, a more equitable treatment from this nation might be obtained for them as well as for us'.

Franklin was taken aback when he bumped into his nemesis, Lord Hillsborough, and was politely invited to spend some time at his Lordship's splendid estate in Co. Down. He stayed for a week but was never quite able to shrug off the feeling that, as he put it himself, 'All the plausible behaviour ... is meant only, by patting and stroking the horse, to make him more patient, while the reins are drawn tighter, and the spurs set deeper into his sides'.

What altered Franklin's attitude to England entirely, and set him on a course that would lead to his endorsement of the American Declaration of Independence in 1776, was a visit to the Irish countryside. There he witnessed the appalling conditions in which the rural Irish lived and the power exercised over them by their landlords.

He wrote that 'their Houses are dirty hovels of mud and straw; their clothing rags, and their food little beside potatoes. Perhaps three fourths of the inhabitants are in this situation'.

He concluded that the Irish economy, governed by the same trade regulations as existed between England and America, would not improve until the tariff regime was changed. This, he believed, was also true of the North American colonies. He also deduced that this would not come about as a result of diplomacy. Franklin left, entirely and reluctantly converted to the conviction that the American colonies would be forced to separate from England. Accordingly, on 4 July 1776, as a Pennsylvanian representative to the Second Continental Congress, he became one of the most prominent signatories of the American Declaration of Independence.

Benjamin Franklin, scientist, philosopher, politician and humanitarian, visited the Irish parliament in Dublin, two hundred and forty-three years ago, on this day.

Broadcast 10 October 2014

2 October 1852
The Journalist and Politician
William O'Brien is Born in Mallow

He was argumentative, controversial, committed, exasperating, vicious, divisive, loyal and lots of other adjectives besides, some positive, some pejorative.

William O'Brien was a poacher turned gamekeeper. For the early part of his life he was a muck-raking nationalist journalist before devoting himself almost entirely to politics. Born into a Cork Fenian family – his brother was a member of the IRB and he may well have been sworn in himself – he was a campaigning newspaperman in his youth in the late 1870s, writing for the stuffy *Freeman's Journal*. Although his often explosive articles got his proprietor, the MP Edmund Dwyer Gray, into plenty of trouble, there was a huge mutual admiration between the Dublin grandee and the Cork firebrand.

In 1881, still in his twenties, he was asked by Charles Stewart Parnell to become the first editor of the new Land League newspaper, *United Ireland*. He took on the task with gusto – so much so that he was arrested and jailed after barely a dozen issues. Totally undeterred, O'Brien continued to edit the newspaper from Kilmainham jail, using the same underground communications system that allowed his leader to continue to conduct his passionate and adulterous relationship with Katharine O'Shea.

After the Land War, *United Ireland* became the mouthpiece of Parnellism and an equal opportunities offender. O'Brien would, on a weekly basis, attack the Liberal and Tory parties in England, the Royal Irish Constabulary and Dublin Metropolitan Police, landlords, unionists, unionist journalists, nationalist journalists who weren't nationalist enough, nationalist MPs who were equally unconvincing in their nationalism and anyone else who, in his eyes, was not stepping up to the mark. On finishing reading the very first issue of *United Ireland* in August 1881, the Chief Secretary for Ireland, William E. Forster, was reported to have asked 'Who is this new madman?'

He was a thorn in the side of the establishment, occasionally of his own party, and arguably he was even a thorn in his own side. He was utterly relentless and fearless in his journalism. That's not to suggest that he was fair – he was anything but. However, he was prepared to risk some stupendous libel suits in order to get his version of the truth out. It helped that for many years he wasn't really worth suing; he had no personal resources and famously lived out of two suitcases in the Imperial Hotel on Sackville Street – later Clery's department store.

Although he could at times be a journalistic windbag, he also had an eye for the pithy phrase or aphorism. When the Tory Prime Minister, Robert Cecil, Lord Salisbury, in 1887 appointed his own nephew Arthur Balfour as Irish Chief Secretary – in the process giving rise to the immortal phrase 'Bob's your uncle' – O'Brien noted the languid Tory's predilection for playing golf and dubbed him 'Mr Arthur Golfour'. Balfour, however, had the last laugh, throwing O'Brien in jail many times over the next four years.

While it broke his heart, he opposed Parnell after the O'Shea divorce case but played little part in the vicious hounding of the former Irish party leader. After Parnell's death in 1891, O'Brien temporarily disappeared from active politics. He re-emerged at the end of the decade to re-assert his dedication to agrarian radicalism by forming the United Irish League. It was under the auspices of this grass roots organisation that the Irish party split was healed. But O'Brien had a penchant for falling out with people and he soon moved on.

His later years as a politician and journalist saw him at the helm of a Cork-based nationalist splinter group, the All For Ireland League, and editing the *Cork Free Press*.

By the time of the 1916 Rising, like many other nationalist politicians of his generation, he had had his day. Although highly respected by many of the more extreme republicans who came to dominate Irish politics post-World War One there was no place for him in the new dispensation and it was time to write a number of highly readable, entertaining and utterly unreliable memoirs. He died in 1928.

William O'Brien, Irish father of the so-called 'New Journalism' of the late nineteenth century, was born in Mallow, Co. Cork, one hundred and sixty-three years ago, on this day.

Broadcast 2 October 2015

16 October 1854
The Birth of Dramatist, Poet and Wit Oscar Wilde

He was born into Victorian Dublin high society with an elaborate set of middle names, these being Fingal O'Flahertie Wills, but it was the two names on either side by which he is better known.

Oscar Wilde was the son of the surgeon Sir William Wilde and the revolutionary nationalist poet Speranza, the pen name of Jane Wilde.

He established himself early in life as a stylish, charismatic aesthete, long before he had proven himself as a writer. He was famous for being famous and this worked to his advantage when he followed the lead of Charles Dickens by travelling to the USA to undergo a lecture tour. This was where he allegedly informed the notoriously humourless US Customs Service that he had nothing to declare but his genius.

He had stumbled into the potentially lucrative tour when Gilbert and Sullivan based the character of Bunthorne in their operetta *Patience* on his eccentricities and striking physical appearance. The promoter Richard d'Oyly Carte decided the American run of *Patience* would do immensely better if it was accompanied by the original. So Bunthorne, aka Oscar, was engaged as a rather striking sandwich-board man for the G&S light opera. He was instructed to cultivate the 'look' of a dandy and address audiences in velvet jacket, knee breeches and with a sunflower in his buttonhole.

The American public, and in particular its press, had never seen anything quite like him before. The *New York World*, curiously claimed that Wilde actually spoke in verse, laying an emphasis on every fourth syllable. Constant reporters' questions varied from the pedestrian to the absolutely bizarre: 'Why was Mr Wilde visiting America? What exactly was meant by aesthetics? At what temperature did he like his bath?'

The New York Fourth estate, a wolf pack with a reputation for savagery, barely laid a glove on the indefatigable Oscar. Their only success related to an apparently harmless question about his trip. This drew from Wilde the laconic observation that the Atlantic Ocean had been something of a disappointment. Predictably, that resulted in the headline 'Wilde disappointed with the Atlantic'. This later prompted a retaliatory letter to a British newspaper signed by 'THE ATLANTIC OCEAN', declaring, 'I am disappointed in Mr Wilde'.

His tour of East Coast cities, where he delivered lectures on the relatively arcane subjects of 'The English Renaissance', 'The House Beautiful' and 'The Decorative Arts' was a huge success. Audiences were more interested in Wilde himself than in anything he might have to say about artistic taste and aesthetics. In many venues young men would show up clad in Wildean costume and mimic his mannerisms.

So successful was Wilde that it was decided to risk touring him in the rather more macho American West, where only the likes of the late and unlamented Colonel George Armstrong Custer or the gunfighter James Butler 'Wild Bill' Hickock had ever been permitted to sport long tresses of hair in the Wilde style. To his chagrin, as the poet journeyed west he discovered pirated and badly-printed volumes of his poetry on sale for ten cents. Copyright editions of his work sold in New York for eight dollars.

His visit to San Francisco – the pearl of the West – was highly and unexpectedly successful. In 1882 the city was barely thirty years old and lacked certain old-world graces. While there, Wilde showed a consummate ability to consume large quantities of alcohol without appearing to suffer the consequences. This stood him in good stead when he was challenged by some members of an exclusive 'gentleman's society', the Bohemian Club. They had decided that this notorious visitor to their city was 'A Miss Nancy' and challenged Oscar to a drinking contest. He drank them all under the table, leaving every last Bohemian drunk in his wake. So impressed were the vanquished San Franciscans that they commissioned a portrait of Wilde and hung it in the club. He did the same thing with a group of miners in Leadville, Colorado. It was here that he spotted the sign he later immortalised: 'please do not shoot the pianist, he is doing his best'.

Oscar Fingal O'Flahertie Wills Wilde, one of whose early career highlights was his lecture tour of the USA, was born, one hundred and sixty-one years ago, on this day.

Broadcast 16 October 2015

31 October 1867
The Death of the Noted Astronomer
the 3rd Earl of Rosse

Once upon a time, Birr, Co. Offaly, didn't exist. There was a town there all right, but it was called Parsonstown, King's County.

The 'Parson' in question wasn't a cleric. The name derived from the Parsons family who were local landowners bearing the hereditary title of Earls of Rosse. The most prominent of that name was the 3rd Earl, William Parsons, born in 1800 during the debate on the Act of Union, a piece of legislation his father vigorously opposed. As the humble Lord Oxmantown, William Parsons had been educated at Trinity College, Dublin and Magdalen College, Oxford, where he graduated with a first in mathematics in 1822. He inherited his father's title in 1841. Prior to that he had been an MP who had voted both for Catholic Emancipation and the Great Reform Bill of 1832.

The facility with hard sums proved to be useful in his future obsession. Because William Parsons was an astronomer. Not just someone who liked to look at the stars through whatever enhancing lens was available, but a serious scientist who won the Royal Medal in 1851. Previous winners included Humphry Davy, John Herschel (three times), Michael Faraday (twice) and our own William Rowan Hamilton. It was a sort of Victorian Nobel Prize.

Once he inherited the title Earl of Rosse and came into possession of Birr Castle, he could do pretty much whatever he liked with the ancestral pile. So he proceeded to move in the biggest telescope ever built – the seventy-two inch 'Leviathan', built to his own specifications. It would continue to be the world's largest telescope, in terms of aperture size, until the early years of the twentieth century. Work on this wonder of modern science and technology began in 1842 and it was completed by 1845. It was constructed largely through trial and error as few telescope makers had left behind the secrets of their trade and, unfortunately, Lord Rosse started out on his labours a century and a half before Google.

'Leviathan' was revealed to the world in a whimsical ceremony. By way of either dedication, blessing or opening, a Church of Ireland Dean walked through the length of the telescope's six-foot wide tube wearing a top hat and with an umbrella raised above his head, presumably just because he could.

No sooner was 'Leviathan' complete than it was rendered inactive by the calamity of the Great Famine. William Parsons devoted much of his family fortune and most of his time for the next three years to alleviating the effects of famine among his tenants.

When Rosse did get 'Leviathan' up and running again his concentration was on the distant nebulae, whose spiral structure he identified thanks to his powerful telescope. He theorised, based on his observations, that millions of galaxies like our own might exist. His conclusions were later borne out when the era of radio-astronomy dawned and his deductions could be verified. Astronomers from all over the world would come to Birr Castle to use 'Leviathan' themselves. Rosse was far from precious when it came to sharing his impressive telescope.

His own findings and theories were published in the proceedings of the Royal Irish Academy and the Royal Astronomical Society. Recognition followed swiftly. Rosse became a Knight of the Order of St Patrick in 1845 and was awarded the French Legion of Honour in 1855.

Rosse's health began to fail in the 1860s and he took a house near the sea at Monkstown, a Dublin suburb, to assist in his recuperation.

William Parsons, the 3rd Earl of Rosse, died, in his home in Monkstown, one hundred and forty-seven years ago, on this day.

Broadcast 31 October 2014

24 October 1878
The Death of Roman Catholic
Prelate Cardinal Paul Cullen

There are those who think of John Charles McQuaid as the most influential and important Irish Roman Catholic Churchman of his time. In terms of his impact on *Irish* society, that may well be the case – he had the ear of Eamon de Valera after all. But another Irish prelate, this one a nineteenth-century Prince of the Church, had the ear of Popes rather than semi-secular parochial potentates. His influence led to his appointment as the first Irish cardinal.

Paul Cullen was born in Kildare in 1803 to a family of prosperous tenant farmers with a history of involvement in extreme nationalist activity. One of his uncles was executed for his part in the 1798 rebellion and his own father was fortunate to avoid the same fate. This was ironic, given Cullen's later obsessive opposition to an oath-bound secret republican organisation, the IRB.

He spent much of his adult life in Rome, where he became Rector of the Irish College and of the much more important College of the Propaganda of the Faith. When radical and often anti-clerical revolutions swept across Europe in 1848, a number of prominent clerics were forced to go 'on the lam' to avoid any unpleasantness and Cullen offered them sanctuary. He managed this by dint of a neat diplomatic trick. He secured the protection of the US Consulate for his palace in Rome. In those days no sane revolutionary would touch a building with the American flag flying overhead – nowadays, of course, they go looking for them. For saving a number of prominent clergymen from untimely and unpleasant deaths, Cullen earned the undying gratitude of Pope Pius IX, who had become pontiff two years before.

Now, if you are going to impress a Pope, it's a good idea to choose one who is embarking on a very long period in office and will have plenty of time to return favours rendered. Such was the case with Pius IX, who had ample opportunity to reward Cullen in a reign of thirty-one years. A record.

Cullen would later ingratiate himself further by helping to raise an Irish Brigade in 1859 to fight in defence of the Papal States against the radical forces of Giuseppe Garibaldi, the only revolutionary to have had a biscuit named after him. The Irish Brigade wasn't much good, neither were the Papal armies. The Pope eventually had to flee Rome in disguise, but that didn't stop Cullen being rewarded with a red hat in 1866.

Cullen first returned to Ireland as Archbishop of Armagh in 1850 and, via the Synod of Thurles the same year, stamped his own considerable authority and reasserted the primacy of Rome and the Pope over the Catholic Church in Ireland. Later he would move to the arch-diocese of Dublin in 1852.

Unlike his equally controversial successor John Charles McQuaid, Cullen largely believed in staying out of politics, although he did oppose the rise of the Young Ireland movement and later that of the Fenians.

His long-running feud with the intensely nationalistic John MacHale, Archbishop of Tuam, became legendary. MacHale had previously conducted an equally long-running fight with Cullen's predecessor in Dublin, Archbishop Murray. He opposed Cullen tooth and nail, one of the principal differences between them being on the issue of papal infallibility. Cullen, more or less, wrote the definition that was accepted by the First Vatican Council in 1870.

MacHale was opposed, though he did not, as James Joyce has one of his characters claim in *Ulysses*, cast his ballot against the measure himself. He had already left Rome in order to avoid having to vote at all.

The pietistic, puritanical and powerful Roman Catholic Church that John Charles McQuaid inherited in 1940 had largely been fashioned by his most illustrious predecessor as Archbishop of Dublin.

Paul Cullen was taken ill and died suddenly, one hundred and thirty-six years ago, on this day.

Broadcast 24 October 2014

9 October 1913
The Birth of Professional Golfer Harry Bradshaw

He was the son of a professional golfer and three of his brothers followed the same calling. Harry Bradshaw was Ireland's first golfing superstar, a proven winner with a jovial personality that endeared him to one and all and helped popularise the professional game in this country.

Bradshaw played golf in the picturesque Delgany Club in Co. Wicklow, where he was treated with respect and admiration. However, this was not always the case where professional golfers were concerned in the 1940s and 50s. Even today, golf would not be noted for its egalitarianism. When Bradshaw was in his pomp it was a thoroughly elitist sport and many of those in its professional ranks were working-class men who often came to the game via the caddying route. They would serve their apprenticeships humping bags for well-heeled club members, sneak in as much practice as was tolerated, become assistant professionals and fix the clubs and shoes of the same members. They would then, if they were fortunate, become fully-fledged professionals and play occasional tournaments for filthy lucre. This did not, of course, entitle them to admission to the Members' Bar. They were, after all, mere employees. To enter the holy of holies they would usually have to be accompanied by a member. There is an enormous social, cultural and sporting gap between Harry Bradshaw and Rory McIlroy.

Bradshaw dominated the Irish professional golfing scene from the time of his first Irish PGA championship victory in 1941. He went on to win it for the next three years, and took first prize ten times in all.

But it was on the international scene that he really made his mark. In the days prior to any notion of a PGA European Tour, the Irish Open championship was a significant event. Brad first won it in 1947 and again two years later. He took the prestigious Dunlop Masters in 1953 and again in 1955. He played on three Ryder Cup teams during this period as well, taking on the Americans in 1953, 1955 and 1957 – the latter event, at Lindrick in England, giving Britain and Ireland its first win in the tournament since 1933.

In 1958, along with Christy O'Connor Senior, he shared in an Irish World Championship victory when they combined to win the Canada Cup – now the World Cup – in Mexico. This was achieved despite the fact that Bradshaw suffered nosebleeds because of the altitude.

But his greatest achievement was also his greatest tragedy. In the 1949 Open Championship at the Royal St George's course in Sandwich in Kent his game was inspired and he took the great South African Bobby Locke to a play-off. It has always been argued that, but for a rush of blood to the head during the second round, Bradshaw would have won that tournament. He had driven off the 5th tee and was walking down the fairway towards his ball when he realised that it had come to rest against a large piece of glass from a broken bottle. He could probably have dropped without penalty, he could well have waited for a ruling, but, somewhat rashly, though in the spirit of the game at the time, he opted to play the ball as it lay and duffed it. Had he been more patient, he might well have won the tournament outright. Sadly, he lost the playoff to Locke, who went on to win three more British Opens.

A few weeks later, in the Irish Open Golf Championship at Belvoir Park in Belfast, Locke was part of a distinguished field. This time, however, Bradshaw had the measure of the great South African and took the trophy. It was revenge of a sort, but scant consolation for his failure to take the British Open. Bradshaw must rank alongside Christy O'Connor Senior as the greatest Irish golfer never to have won a Major. However, his heyday was at a time when the notion of 'Majors' was not as well developed as it is now and it was virtually impossible for Irish pros to play in the big money tournaments in the USA.

Harry Bradshaw, the ebullient, trailblazing Irish professional golfer, was born in Delgany, Co. Wicklow, one hundred and two years ago, on this day.

Broadcast 9 October 2015

November

Minister McEntee, jazzing the Budget

14 November 1669
Oliver Plunkett Becomes
Archbishop of Armagh

To generations of Irish children his is the rather frightening head that stares out of a glass shrine in St Peter's Roman Catholic Church in Drogheda, Co. Louth. Even if you knew what to expect as a child it was a memorable sight – probably the stuff of many a subsequent nightmare.

But before Oliver Plunkett became separated from his head at the behest of elements of the British establishment on 1 July 1681, he had been a distinguished cleric, educated on the continent during the time of the Penal Laws and functioning at a high level in Rome before his appointment in 1669 to the See of Armagh.

Plunkett had been born in Loughcrew, near Oldcastle in Co. Meath to well-to-do parents of Anglo-Norman stock. By the time of his appointment as Primate of Ireland, attitudes towards Roman Catholic priests had relaxed sufficiently to allow him to take up his position.

He was a reforming Archbishop. He found Irish priests to be sadly 'ignorant in moral theology', though their lack of such knowledge may have had much to do with their inability to acquire a grounding in philosophy while trying to avoid being executed or tarred and feathered at the hands of the authorities in the mid-1600s. The new archbishop also took on drunkenness among members of the clergy, observing that if this habit was squashed, Irish priests would become saints. As it turned out, he himself was the only Irish cleric of the period to be canonised.

In 1678 Plunkett fell victim to the infamous English Popish Plot of the notorious perjurer Titus Oates, who fabricated knowledge of a Catholic conspiracy to murder King Charles II. Oates shopped the Archbishop by alleging that he had evidence of Plunkett colluding to bring twenty thousand French soldiers to Ireland. Plunkett might have chosen discretion and headed back to Rome, but instead he insisted on remaining in Ireland, though he, sensibly, went on the run. He was captured and tried in Dundalk, where numerous informers came forward to confirm the charges against him. The Lord Lieutenant of the day, the Duke of Ormonde, privately referred to them as 'silly drunken vagabonds whom no schoolboy would trust to rob an orchard'. The trial quickly collapsed so Plunkett was brought to London to face charges there instead. A grand jury found no case against him, but he continued to be detained until the Crown could find witnesses who would stitch him up with the help of a co-operative judge, in this case the Lord Chief Justice, Sir Francis Pemberton.

Plunkett was found guilty of 'promoting the Roman faith' in June 1681 – which was probably a fair cop, though was far from plotting regicide. The penalty, however, was the same in both cases, and on 1 July 1681, the incumbent Roman Catholic Archbishop of Armagh became the last Catholic martyr to die in England, when he was hanged, drawn and quartered at Tyburn. In case you are wondering what is involved in the ancient practice of hanging, drawing and quartering, believe me, you don't want to know.

His head eventually found its way to Rome, went from there to Armagh before being installed in Drogheda. Most of his body was interred in Downside Abbey in Somerset. That's Down*side* Abbey, it's actually the real thing, a monastery, unlike the fictional home of the fictional Crawley family.

   Since his death, Plunkett's trial has been described by many distinguished British jurists as an egregious miscarriage of justice, even by seventeenth century standards.

   Oliver Plunkett, canonised in 1975, was appointed to the See of Armagh, three hundred and forty-five years ago, on this day.

Broadcast 14 November 2014

13 November 1775
General Richard Montgomery Takes Montreal at the Head of an American Force

The Fenians were not the only Irish-led force to invade Canada – they tried unsuccessfully five times in the 1860s. Almost a century beforehand another Irish-born general did so – Richard Montgomery – at the head of an army of the American revolution. In so doing, Montgomery was putting himself at odds with his former employers as his training had been in the British army.

Montgomery was born in Swords, Co. Dublin, in 1738, although his family had a Donegal background. He spent his early years in Abbeville House in Kinsealy – the name may be familiar. It was subsequently owned by another Irishman of northern origins who had his own problems with our nearest neighbours, one Charles J. Haughey. Although Montgomery spent two years in Trinity College he didn't graduate. Instead he took a commission in the British army a few months shy of his eighteenth birthday.

His first assignment was, inevitably, fighting the French – on this occasion in North America. In 1760 he was involved in the capture of Montreal from France. Three years later he was back in America fighting against the Ottawa nation and its military leader, Pontiac – today better known as an automobile.

By the early 1770s Montgomery had left the army and returned to North America where he settled down, married and began life as a farmer. Having married into the prominent New York Livingston family, Montgomery began to see himself as an American rather than an Anglo-Irish emigrant. From that he graduated to becoming a fully-fledged 'patriot' – taking the American side in the many rancorous disputes that arose with the British Crown around this time.

With the formation of the Continental army under George Washington in 1775, Montgomery was pressed into service as a Brigadier General and given charge of a New York brigade with orders to invade Canada. It would be a case of *déjà vu* for the Irish general. His force was to be joined by another, from Maine, led by General Benedict Arnold. This is where timing is all-important. Benedict Arnold's is a name still reviled today in the USA. In 1780 he would become as popular in America as was Thierry Henry in this country in 2009. Henry merely handled a football at an inappropriate moment; Arnold plotted to hand over Westpoint to the British. The plan failed and he legged it. But in 1775 he was still on the American side.

After some initial successes in Canada, Montgomery opted for a return to Montreal – you could call it *déjà vu* all over again except, of course, that would be tautology. Hearing of his approach, the British defenders of the city boarded a number of small ships and fled down the St Lawrence river. The city was taken without a shot being fired.

The next target was Quebec. On the march from Montreal to that city, Montgomery was joined by the forces of Benedict Arnold. The future traitor handed over his command to the Irishman. The men from Maine by this time were a sorry sight, having endured much on their march into French-speaking Canada.

Montgomery wanted Quebec too to surrender without a fight. A letter offering generous terms was despatched and duly burnt by the British army commander General Guy Carleton. When Montgomery sent a messenger with the same offer to local businesses he was arrested by Carleton. Not discouraged, the Irish general simply delivered his message to the people of Quebec by having it attached to an arrow and fired over the walls into the city. Answer came there none – so Quebec was first bombarded and then assaulted. Unfortunately, Montgomery, who was leading the attack, was killed by a blast of grapeshot to the head. Unknown to himself he had been promoted to Major General prior to the assault on Quebec. Benedict Arnold took over the patriot forces – which to an American is a bit like Vladimir Putin assuming charge of the CIA.

Richard Montgomery, at the head of an American Patriot army, took the Canadian city of Montreal, two hundred and forty years ago, on this day.

Broadcast 13 November 2015

27 November 1857
The Birth of Surgeon and Explorer
Thomas H. Parke

Nestling in the grounds of the Natural History Museum in Dublin, on a lawn in front of the much-loved 'Dead Zoo', is the statue of an Irish surgeon. On a bronze plaque on the pedestal is depicted the image of two men in what might appear to be an intimate moment. One is in fact a surgeon and he is in the act of sucking poison from an arrow wound in the chest of the other.

The man doing the sucking (one hesitates to describe him as a 'sucker') is an Irish physician named Thomas H. Parke. The 'suckee', who survived to tell the tale of how he might well have died from a native African arrow in August 1887, was one Captain William Stairs. Both men were, at the time, employed on an expedition by the notorious explorer, adventurer, coloniser and opportunist William Morton Stanley, the man reputed to have uttered the immortal words 'Dr Livingstone, I presume' and who then proceeded to rape much of central Africa at the behest of genocidal European monarchs like King Leopold of Belgium.

Thomas H. Parke was born in Clogher House in Kilmore, Co. Roscommon, in 1857, and brought up mostly in Carrick on Shannon in Co. Leitrim. He attended the College of Surgeons in Dublin and joined the British army as a medical officer in 1881. Much of his military career was spent in Africa. He served in Egypt and was with the column that belatedly fought its way to the non-relief of the ill-fated and already deceased General Gordon in Khartoum in 1885.

But it was his association with Stanley that brought him fame and a modicum of fortune – though not from his boss. He enlisted as medical officer on one of Stanley's infamous ventures – the so-called Relief of Emin Pasha Expedition. It was part of the fallout of the Gordon debacle and emanated from pressure on the British government not to repeat the delay in sending assistance to the beleaguered Gordon in Sudan.

When Parke offered his services they were, at first, rejected. But he was quickly taken on anyway under not very generous terms. He was to receive an allowance of forty pounds for the purchase of suitable clothing, fifteen pounds for medical supplies and no pay for three years. Stanley recorded at the time that Parke was 'an extremely handsome young gentleman, diffident somewhat, but extremely prepossessing'. Parke also had to sign a non-disclosure clause. There was to be no best-selling memoir until six months after the official report of the expedition was published. In other words, he was to remain silent until Stanley had taken all the credit for any successes and made a small fortune from publishing his account of the expedition.

Parke didn't have an easy time of it. There was an early outbreak of smallpox which he had to deal with. Then there was the matter of his accommodation. This he shared with the twelve wives of an Arab expeditionary, Tippu-Tib. He appears to have had difficulty in tactfully pointing out to their doubtless adoring husband that the standards of hygiene in his harem might have been higher. The expedition spent thirty-three months in the African interior, during which time Parke reckoned – in the memoir he was eventually permitted to write – that each of the Europeans experienced at least one hundred and fifty attacks of malaria. So he was a busy man.

He must also have been conscious that, although he had the distinction of being the first Irishman to traverse the continent of Africa, he was also travelling through a region where the native population, in times of need, were prone to the practice known as 'facultative anthropophagy' – in other words, to you and me, they were cannibals. Attacks on the expedition were regular and many members were lost to disease and military action.

During his three years in the interior Parke purchased a pygmy girl – not the sort of thing they're used to in Roscommon. She helped him through his own frequent bouts of malaria but the relationship, whatever its precise nature, ended when he was forced to leave her in the forest as her eyes were unable to adapt to the sunlight of the coastal regions.

Stanley thought very highly indeed of Parke – something of a mixed blessing – as, no doubt, did the man whose life he saved in 1887, William Stairs. He did get to publish a memoir after returning home. The snappily titled *My Personal Experiences in Equatorial Africa*, was published in 1891. The more influential *A Guide to Health in Africa* followed shortly after.

They did, by the way, find Emin Pasha, a German physician, who apparently was getting on just fine thank you and didn't need to be rescued. Stanley sold one hundred and fifty thousand copies of his memoirs before he came under fire for presiding over the deaths of hundreds of his men in yet another spurious 'smash and grab' effort in Africa.

Parke did not long outlive the end of the expedition. He died in 1893 and is buried in Drumsna in Co. Leitrim.

Thomas H. Parke, surgeon, soldier and naturalist, was born, one hundred and fifty-eight years ago, on this day.

Broadcast 27 November 2015

28 November 1871
The Gaiety Theatre Opens in Dublin

It has become known as the 'Old Lady of South King Street'. The Gaiety is now a venerable theatre that has managed to survive some lean times and very stiff competition. In 1871, however, it was brand-new, luxurious, well-appointed, and it accommodated almost two thousand people, seven hundred in the pit and stalls, two hundred in the balcony, two hundred and ten in the upper circle, and a further seven hundred in the gallery. The gallery was known to one and all as 'The Gods' because the seats were closer to Heaven than they were to the stage and the patrons required the eyesight and hearing of an all-powerful deity to follow what was going on many metres below them.

Despite competition from the Olympia, which opened eight years later, and other sizeable venues like the Theatre Royal, the Gaiety quickly became a fixture on the Dublin scene, attracting many visiting companies such as that of the great actor-manager Henry Irving and the d'Oyly Carte Opera, spiritual and contractual home of the works of Gilbert and Sullivan.

The Gaiety was not unaffected by the various excitements of the revolutionary decade. During the Easter Rising, members of the Rathmines and Rathgar Musical Society, another bi-annual tenant, had been 'trapped' in the Shelbourne Hotel by the hostilities. There are, it has to be said, far worse places to be imprisoned, and the Shelbourne was out of range of the revolver prominently sported and rebelliously employed by the excitable Countess Markievicz around St Stephen's Green during the rebellion. At least the R&R was only in rehearsal. The d'Oyly Carte had already arrived in force for their traditional Easter week shows at the Gaiety when Pearse, Connolly, Plunkett and units of the Irish Volunteers and the Irish Citizen's Army took over the GPO. As fortune would have it the Gilbert and Sullivan players and stage crew had been booked into the Gresham Hotel across the road in Sackville Street for the week. Discretion proving to be much the better part of valour, the company members never left the hotel and the Gaiety, sadly, did not ring to the strains of *I am the very model of a modern major general* or *A policeman's lot is not a happy one* that Easter.

Two names are most associated with the theatre. Louis Elliman, son of Russian-Jewish parents, bought the theatre in 1936 and held it for almost thirty years. The Gaiety was only one of Elliman's entertainment interests. He also had an association with the Theatre Royal and later co-founded Ardmore Studios with World War One and Irish Civil War veteran Emmet Dalton in 1958. The following year his main theatrical venue was mired in controversy involving, naturally enough, the Roman Catholic Archbishop of Dublin, John Charles McQuaid and the staging of an adaptation of J. P. Donleavy's controversial novel *The Gingerman*. The stage version of the novel, due for a two-week run, was pulled after three nights. According to Donleavy himself, Elliman was visited by McQuaid's private secretary who requested, or advised him, to close the show down. Elliman opted to comply rather than take on the crozier.

Were it not for the intervention of the second saviour of the Old Lady of South King Street in 1965, the Gaiety might now be an office block or a very expensive car park.

The venue faced stiff competition, not just from other theatres but from cinema and television too. In the final five years of the reign of Louis Elliman, only seven productions turned a profit for the Gaiety management. Elliman died in November 1965 at the age of fifty-nine. The Gaiety, fortunate to survive as a theatre, was sold in 1966 and was, at the time of its centenary, being run by Eamon Andrews Studios in the shape of the redoubtable Fred O'Donovan, a worthy successor to Elliman. He held the reins for almost twenty years and, with the help of Maureen Potter, heir to the great Jimmy O'Dea, the Gaiety survived.

In its latter years one of the theatre's most entertaining, if bizarre, moments was when it re-opened after refurbishment with a 'Night of A Hundred Stars' in October 1984. One of those stars was either an idiosyncratic or intoxicated Peter O'Toole, whose five-minute slot reading an extract from Swift's *Modest Proposal* morphed into a twenty-minute rendition of the entire essay. This led to hisses, catcalls and walk-outs from members of the well-heeled audience. They were either offended by the Hollywood star's invocation of eighteenth-century Dublin poverty, or bored by the length of time it took him to read the viciously satirical piece, advocating the fattening and slaughter for profit of babies by impecunious Dubliners as a handy source of revenue.

The Gaiety Theatre opened its doors for the first time, one hundred and forty-three years ago, on this day.

Broadcast on 28 November 2014

7 November 1878
The Birth of Suffragist and First Female Magistrate in India, Margaret Cousins

It was Clare-woman Georgina Frost who, after a long legal campaign, became the first woman to occupy a paid position in the UK legal establishment, that of Petty Sessions clerk. That was in 1919, but it took an appeal to the House of Lords to secure the post that she then had to give up in 1922 when the new Free State government abolished Petty Sessions in a reform of the Irish legal system.

Of just as much interest is Margaret Cousins, who became the first female magistrate in 1922. Cousins was born Margaret Gillespie, in 1878, into a highly respectable middle-class family in Boyle, Co. Roscommon. She was to have been a professional music teacher, but fate had other things in mind for her.

In the early 1900s she discovered feminism, became a convinced suffragist and formed, along with Hannah Sheehy Skeffington and others, the Irish Women's Franchise League. And she was far from being a faint-hearted suffragist at that. She was an enthusiastic wielder of the weapon of choice for Irish women suffragists, the small carpenter's hammer, and was frequently known to toss same at the target of choice, the windows of individuals, organisations or government agencies felt by the Irish Woman's Franchise League to thoroughly deserve such unwelcome attention.

Her unerring accuracy and fearsome right arm earned her a couple of periods of detention at the Lord Lieutenant's pleasure in Mountjoy and Tullamore prisons. There she demanded political status and went on hunger strike to back up her demands. In England suffragists on hunger strike meant only one thing – forced feeding. The Irish authorities, however, proved a tad more reasonable and Cousins and her fellow IWFL members got more or less what they wanted.

When it came to dealing with the Irish Parliamentary Party, however, this was not the case. Attempts were made to include votes for women in the Home Rule Bill, but John Redmond let it be known that such a move would happen over his dead body. Unfortunately for Margaret Cousins, when Redmond's demise did take place, she was in India with her husband James.

Not that removal to India in any way dampened her enthusiasm for the female suffrage campaign. She helped found the Indian Women's Association in 1917 and demanded that the issue be on the agenda of the burgeoning Indian independence movement. In 1922, at a time when women were finally being called to the bar in Ireland and Britain, she became the first female magistrate in India, or anywhere else in the British Empire for that matter.

You would have thought that such a promotion would have ended the radical career of Margaret Cousins. Not a bit of it. While still a magistrate she was arrested in 1932 for a protest against free speech and sentenced to a year in jail. While in prison she organised another hunger strike in support of Mahatma Gandhi. After her release she continued to be a thorn in the side of the Imperial administration, despite a stroke, right up to the granting of Indian independence in 1948. She died, at the age of seventy-five, in 1954.

Incidentally, she also put her musical talents to good use. She is credited with composing, in 1919, the melody for what became the Indian national anthem.

Margaret Cousins, Gretta to her friends, was born in Boyle, one hundred and thirty-six years ago, on this day.

Broadcast 7 November 2014

21 November 1915
Shackleton's *Endurance* Sinks

It all started out with high expectations. The title was the rather grandiose 'The Imperial Trans-Antarctic Expedition', but the idea was simple: for a team led by Irish explorer Ernest Shackleton to cross the Antarctic continent. Funded by the British government and many individual donors, including Scottish jute merchant James Caird, the expedition was given the go-ahead in August 1914, despite the outbreak of war a few days before the scheduled departure.

Shackleton's ship, the *Endurance*, one of two making the journey, was captained by Frank Worsley. An Irishman, Tom Crean, looked after the seventy dogs on board with names like Slobbers, Painful, Shakespeare, Bummer and even Amundsen, who were expected to haul the explorers and their equipment across the ice.

But it all went drastically wrong when, in early 1915, the *Endurance* was encased in an ice floe and inexorably crushed to destruction. She had already been abandoned when, in November 1915, she sank below the surface, an episode recorded by the movie camera of the expedition's Australian photographer Frank Hurley.

Shackleton managed to get his crew to Elephant Island, almost three hundred and fifty miles from where the *Endurance* had gone down. But the chances of rescue were slim. The celebrated decision was then taken to launch the small lifeboat, named the *James Caird*, after the donor whose money had helped create the predicament, and for six members of the crew, led by Shackleton, to try and find help. Making the journey in April 1916 with the famous explorer were two fellow Irishmen: Kerryman Tom Crean and able seaman Timothy McCarthy from Cork.

Taking only four weeks' supplies of food, Shackleton pointed the *James Caird* in the direction of South Georgia, more than eight hundred miles away. The navigational skills of the *Endurance* captain, Frank Worlsey, ensured that the small craft managed to reach its destination after fifteen days, but it was forced to land on the southern shore of the island. Help, in the form of a Norwegian whaling station, was far to the north.

This opened the next chapter of the unlikely rescue of the crew of the *Endurance*. Shackleton opted to go over land, across forbidding mountains in freezing temperatures, in a journey that had never been attempted before. He took Worsley and Crean with him. Famously, after thirty-six hours, they made it to the Stromness whaling station, on 20 May 1916, to the absolute astonishment of the Norwegian occupants of this isolated outpost of civilisation. It was another forty years before British explorer Duncan Carse emulated the achievement of Shackleton, Crean and Worsley.

It was not until August 1916 that the explorer was able to rescue the bulk of the original *Endurance* crew and bring them all to safety.

When Shackleton returned to civilisation, one of the first questions he asked was about the final outcome of the war that had just broken out when he and his crew had left for the South Pole. He was shocked to be informed that the outcome was still to be decided. The Great War, already two years old, would continue for a further two years and three months.

The *Endurance*, after being slowly crushed by ice for ten months, finally succumbed and sank, ninety-nine years ago on this day.

Broadcast 21 November 2014

20 November 1925
Commissioner Eoin MacNeill
Resigns from the Boundary
Commission

It's not widely known, but, at one point during the twentieth century, Ireland was actually a thirty-two county independent state. However, that particular union lasted just over twenty-four hours. It came about in the first place when the Irish Free State was formally established on 6 December 1922. At that point Northern Ireland was obliged to formally secede from a united Ireland. That didn't happen until 8 December.

Under Article 12 of the Anglo-Irish Treaty, signed in December 1921, it had been agreed that if Northern Ireland did decide to opt out of the Irish Free State, a three-person commission would meet to decide on the final boundary between the two new political entities. As the border areas were predominantly nationalist, it was assumed by the Free State government that the reallocation of land would all be in one direction, from north to south, and would be on a sizeable scale.

The Irish Civil War intervened so that the establishment of the Boundary Commission had to wait until 1924. Its job was to 'determine in accordance with the wishes of the inhabitants, so far as may be compatible with economic and geographic conditions

the boundaries between Northern Ireland and the rest of Ireland.'
So a pretty woolly brief to begin with.

The British government appointed a South African judge,
Richard Feetham, to chair the body. The Irish appointee was
Minister for Education Eoin MacNeill, he of 1916 'countermanding
order' fame, while the Northern Ireland administration, led by
James Craig, flatly refused to play ball and appoint anyone. The
two other governments therefore made the appointment for them
and Belfast barrister and newspaper editor Joseph Fisher became
the third member of the Commission.

The meetings of the Boundary Commission were held *in camera*
and no one knew precisely what they were up to until a leak to the
Tory newspaper, *The Morning Post,* in November 1925. This was
said to have come via Fisher and put the Dublin government in an
awkward position. It revealed that the traffic was not all going to be
one way. The Commissioners, while transferring two hundred and
eighty-six square miles from north to south, were recommending
that seventy-seven square miles go in the opposite direction, from
East Donegal to Derry. Which technically is, of course, west to
east, but you know what I mean.

The leak meant that it became time to shelve the findings of the
Boundary Commission and seek a way of bypassing the terms of the
Treaty. This was achieved with an interesting piece of misdirection.
First MacNeill resigned as the Free State Commissioner and then
a deal was done with the government of Stanley Baldwin – it was
a trade-off that worked to this State's economic benefit, whatever
about the outcome for Northern nationalists. A controversial
element of the Anglo-Irish Treaty was the agreement of the Free
State to make a continued contribution toward the UK public
debt. In 1924 this amounted to seven billion pounds and Ireland's
share of the cost of servicing the debt (which had not been paid
for the duration of the Civil War) was reckoned to be anywhere
between five and nineteen million pounds a year.

This was at a time when the annual Irish government budget came to just twenty-five million pounds. The Free State agreed to leave border Catholics in Northern Ireland in exchange for not having to pony up to pay off British debt. During the Dáil debate on the measure a delegation of Northern nationalists sought to make representations to the government on this new agreement but were not given access.

Many years later Spike Milligan made the labours of the Boundary Commission an integral part of his hilarious comic novel *Puckoon*. Milligan has the Commission draw the border right through the middle of the village of Puckoon. Most is apportioned to the Free State but a good slice ends up in Northern Ireland. This, however, far from being entirely negative, has certain advantages for the inhabitants. The town's public house, for example, is bisected by the border. This means that drink is thirty per cent cheaper in one jurisdiction and the licensing hours are longer in the other. So the patrons buy all their pints in Northern Ireland and then crowd into the other half of the bar when the Northern part closes down for the night.

Eoin MacNeill, Minister for Education in the Free State government, resigned from the Boundary Commission after an embarrassing leak to the *Morning Post*, ninety years ago, on this day.

Broadcast 20 November 2015

6 November 1929
The Gaelic League Bans
'Foreign Dances'

We are a nation given to bans and boycotts. The latter expression, famously, has its origins in the Land War of the early 1880s. For many years the Gaelic Athletic Association maintained a ban on members playing soccer, rugby, hockey and cricket. During the so-called 'Economic War' of the 1930s we were encouraged to 'burn everything English except their coal' – a phrase that dates back to Jonathan Swift in the 1720s. But few campaigns can have been as bizarre as the hysterical antipathy towards jazz music in the 1920s and 30s.

The Great War, in which millions died, was, not unnaturally, followed by a period of anti-establishment moral and political lassitude. On the basis of what had gone on between 1914-18, many young European and American citizens chose to spend the next decade operating on the basis of the axiom 'eat, drink and be merry for tomorrow we die'. The trenches and industrialised killing gave way to the Charleston, bobbed hair and shorter skirts. It was, to many older citizens who had spent the war in their clubs and drawing rooms, the collapse of civilisation as they knew it. Critics of modern music and dance saw nothing particularly untoward in mass slaughter but were appalled at the excesses of the depraved Black Bottom and incendiary jazz music.

In post-war Ireland, mass unemployment, abject poverty and wholesale emigration seemed to be of less significance to our legislators and the Roman Catholic hierarchy than stopping people listening and, far worse, dancing, to the devil's music. The Cumann na nGaedhal government even set up a committee of investigation (the Carrigan Committee) which consulted expert witnesses on how the morality of the Irish youth might be safeguarded against such corrupting foreign influences as Louis Armstrong and Glen Miller.

Co. Leitrim emerged as the last bastion of Gaelic civilisation when the parish priest of the village of Cloone, Father Peter Conferey, lambasted jazz from the pulpit and urged people to sing Irish songs and wear home-spun clothing only. A demonstration under the auspices of the Gaelic League was organised in nearby Mohill. It was reported to have been attended by three thousand people, some of whom carried banners with slogans such as 'Down with Jazz' and 'Out with Paganism'. A supportive message was read at the meeting from the Catholic Primate of Ireland, Cardinal McRory, who described jazz dancing as 'suggestive … demoralising [and] a fruitful source of scandal and of ruin'. The Cardinal speculated that listening to such debauched music had been 'the occasion of irreparable disgrace and life-long sorrow' for many young Irish women. Given that jazz had been barely a decade in Ireland, the 'lifelong' bit was probably something of a stretch.

At the same meeting the Secretary of the Gaelic League, Sean Óg O'Ceallaigh, attacked no less a personage than the rather ascetic Fianna Fáil Minister for Finance Sean McEntee. He was condemned for permitting Radio Éireann to play jazz music occasionally. O'Ceallaigh said, rather improbably, of the austere McEntee that 'Our Minister for Finance has a soul buried in jazz and is selling the musical soul of the nation […] He is jazzing every night of the week.'

In January 1934 the *Leitrim Observer* fulminated editorially against what it called 'Saxon' influences. 'Let the pagan Saxon be

276

told that we Irish Catholics do not want and will not have the dances and the music that he has borrowed from the savages of the islands of the Pacific'. The racist theme was later taken up by Fr Conefrey when he described jazz as being 'borrowed from the language of the savages of Africa' – so quite a geographical spread there. He then went on to attack An Garda Siochána, insisting that many members of the force were guilty of organising depraved all night jazz dances. A far cry indeed from the Policeman's Ball.

The campaign had the effect of forcing the introduction of the 1935 Dance Halls Act, requiring all those who wished to organise such an event to apply for a licence. This, ironically, had the side-effect of making Irish traditional dances in rural homes illegal. Be careful what you wish for.

The Gaelic League decreed that anyone attending 'foreign' dances where jazz music was played, risked expulsion, eighty-six years ago, on this day.

Broadcast 6 November 2015

December

An Irish solution

18 December 1878
The Hanging of John 'Black Jack' Kehoe of the Molly Maguires

Their Irish origins are mysterious, though they were almost definitely a nineteenth-century agrarian secret society. Their name may have emanated from a tradition that was not just Irish – the Welsh were party to it as well in the so-called Rebecca Riots – where male activists disguised themselves as women before engaging in illegal activity up to and including murder. They may have also have been associated with the main Roman Catholic rival to the Orange Order, the Ancient Order of Hibernians.

But it wasn't in Ireland that the Molly Maguires made a name for themselves. It was in the anthracite mines and on the rail-roads of Pennsylvania. Here, the tactics used against landlords and land agents in Ireland were applied in bitter labour disputes, with the Ancient Order of Hibernians, an organisation that originated in the USA, acting as a legitimate front for the illegal activities of the Mollies. Then again, there are historians who do not believe this shadowy conspiracy ever existed on the scale that was claimed by the owners and shareholders of the mines and railways in late nineteenth-century Pennsylvania. That is a point of view that was widely held at the time as well.

Immigrant labour offered a glorious opportunity for Pennsylvania capitalists to undercut the wages being paid to

American-born miners. Wages for Irish migrants were low and conditions were brutal. 'On the job' fatalities and injuries ran into the hundreds each year. The so-called 'panic of 1873' – not a million miles removed from the Wall Street Crash of 1929 and the 'sub-prime' crisis of 2007 made a bad situation even worse for the mine and railroad workers.

Just as every crisis brings opportunity, mostly for the unscrupulous, the President of the Philadelphia and Reading Coal and Iron company, Franklin Gowen, son of an Irish immigrant and the richest man in the region, decided it was high time to crush the burgeoning trade union activity in the state, represented by the Workingmen's Benevolent Association. While the 'Molly Maguires' may have been the convenient invention of Gowen himself, there is no doubt that perceived enemies of the Pennsylvania mineworkers were being killed by the dozen. In one of the six main anthracite-mining counties there had been fifty such murders between 1863-67.

Gowen, with the co-operation of his fellow mine owners, engaged the services of the yet-to-be-famous Pinkerton detective agency run by Scottish immigrant Allan Pinkerton, to help break a general strike in the anthracite fields. In 1875 he despatched an agent, Armagh-born James McParland, to the area. Posing as 'James McKenna', the Pinkerton detective infiltrated the Benevolent Association and claimed also to have insinuated himself into the confidence of the Molly Maguires. Information gathered by McParland was, in the first instance, passed on to vigilante elements who happened to share Gowen's union-bashing objectives. When suspected 'Mollies' were murdered in their own homes, McParland threatened to resign from the Pinkerton organisation but was persuaded to remain in place. After six months the strike ended and most of the miners returned to work, having agreed to a twenty per cent wage cut. However, Irish-born members of the Ancient Order of Hibernians refused to concede and fought on. Attacks on overseers, strike-breakers and police continued until information supplied by McParland led to a number of arrests.

The Armagh Pinkerton, who had, by his own account, been a trusted collaborator of the leadership of the Mollies, testified against a number of those accused of murder. Demonstrating the extent of his political power within the state of Pennsylvania, Gowen managed to have himself made special prosecutor and actually conducted some of the cases against the Mollies. The accused included the alleged ringleader of the organisation, John 'Black Jack' Kehoe. McParland's testimony sent ten men to the gallows. Many of them, including Kehoe, loudly proclaimed their innocence of the crimes of which they had been convicted. In 1979 the state of Pennsylvania pardoned Kehoe posthumously after an investigation by its Board of Pardons at the behest of one of his descendants.

The Molly Maguires have passed into legend. Arthur Conan Doyle based a Sherlock Holmes mystery, *The Valley of Fear,* on their alleged activities. The 1970 film, *The Molly Maguires*, starred Sean Connery as Kehoe and Richard Harris as McParland.

John 'Black Jack' Kehoe, the last, and most prominent, of the Molly Maguire defendants, was hanged in Pennsylvania, one hundred and thirty-seven years ago, on this day.

Broadcast 18 December 2015

4 December 1879
The Birth of Composer
Hamilton Harty

How do you respond to the description 'the prince of accompanists'? With delight if you want to spend your working life playing piano chords while an opera or *lieder* singer performs downstage of you and takes all the accolades. But perhaps not so ardently if your ambition in life is to be a composer and conductor.

The Irish composer Hamilton Harty, born in Hillsborough, Co. Down in 1879, was so described by the *Musical Times* in 1920. He was something of a musical prodigy – he became a church organist in rural Co. Antrim at the age of twelve and held down similar posts in Belfast, and Bray, Co. Wicklow while still a teenager. He moved to London in his early twenties where he was seen as a 'promising composer and outstanding accompanist' – there it is again, second fiddle.

However, he was good enough as a composer to have his *Comedy Overture* performed at the 1907 Proms by an orchestra under the direction of Sir Henry Wood himself. In addition, he didn't do too badly out of being an accompanist in that one of the soloists with whom he worked was the soprano Anges Nicholls. She later became Mrs Harty.

As a composer he devoted much of his time to reworking traditional Irish themes. This is evident in his *Irish Symphony*, first performed at the Feis Ceoil in Dublin in 1904 with Harty himself conducting. That same year the third place finisher in the singing competition was one James Joyce.

Harty also began conducting with the London Symphony Orchestra in 1911. In 1913 he conducted the orchestra in his own composition *Variations on a Dublin Air*. He was also invited to conduct at Covent Garden around that time but Harty and grand opera never really hit it off. The composer wrote of opera that it was a medium in which 'clumsy attempts are made at defining the indefinable suggestions of music'. There is no record of what opera thought of Harty, but the *Times* wrote that his efforts made the music of Bizet and Wagner sound like 'quotations from some forgotten German score'. Ouch!

Harty finally found his niche as a conductor with the Hallé Orchestra in Manchester. He made his debut with the Hallé in April 1914. Unfortunately his career was interrupted by the small matter of a global war. He sensibly joined the Navy, where casualties were considerably lighter than on dry land and survived to be demobilised in 1918. He became the permanent conductor of the Hallé in 1920 and restored the reputation of the orchestra to the levels it had experienced under its founder, Charles Hallé.

Harty and the Hallé came to fit each other like a pair of old gloves. On one occasion the famous Austrian pianist Artur Schnabel was performing a Brahms concerto with the Hallé. He overlooked two bars, enough to throw any conductor and orchestra into total confusion. Harty and the Hallé didn't so much as miss a beat. Later Schnabel, by way of a compliment to the conductor, suggested that the Hallé was 'second only to the Berlin Philharmonic'. Harty was having none of it – pointing out with some asperity that the Hallé was 'better by two bars'.

Harty was knighted in 1925 but his career in Manchester did not come to a happy end. When, in 1932, he accepted the post of conductor in chief with the London Symphony Orchestra, the Hallé dropped him like a hot bassoon. He took some measure of revenge by poaching a number of their key players for his new band. However, his tenure with the LSO was brief and chastening. He didn't bring in the crowds and was dumped unceremoniously after only two years.

Towards the end of his life he suffered ill health but still managed to adapt a number of Irish songs and create a new tone poem, 'The Children of Lir'. He did a lot of work in his final years with the BBC Symphony Orchestra. He was only sixty-one when he died in 1940. His ashes were scattered in Hillsborough parish church.

Hamilton Harty, accompanist, composer, and conductor, was born one hundred and thirty-six years ago, on this day.

Broadcast 4 December 2015

12 December 1883
The Birth of Composer
Peadar Kearney

It's probably the only song in existence whose lyrics are known by the majority of the Irish people in the first national language. When was the last time you were at an international soccer match or a significant Gaelic Games event and heard anyone signing the lyrics 'Soldiers are we, whose lives are pledged to Ireland' as opposed to 'Sine Fianna Fáil atá faoi gheall ag Eirinn'?

This affiliation to the Irish language version, as we will see, diminishes somewhat the acceptance of Peadar Kearney as the writer of the Irish National anthem. Kearney is the author of the lyrics of 'The Soldier's Song', which was adopted by the Irish Free State in July 1926 as our national anthem. It is said in some circles to have replaced 'God Save Ireland' by Timothy Daniel Sullivan as the national anthem of the fledgling Irish state. However, this is a myth; despite the iconic status of 'God Save Ireland', it was never formally adopted as anything other than a rousing, defiant, and frequently-sung republican hymn. 'A Nation Once Again' probably has equal claims to being the precursor of 'The Soldier's Song', but the Irish Free State did not move to adopt a national anthem of any kind until 1926.

Neither is it entirely clear if the lyrics and music of the song, or just the melody itself, constitute the Irish national anthem. Or whether anything other than the chorus has official status. Kearney was not really responsible for the melody, this was largely written by frequent collaborator Patrick Heeney to Kearney's lyrics. The other problem is that the English language version has been almost entirely superseded by the Irish translation, 'Amhrán na bhFiann', written by Liam O'Rinn in 1923. When the song was played at the Ryder Cup in the USA in 2004 in its English language form it caused something of a storm in a tin cup. Confusion also reigned in 1994 when an American band played the utterly unfamiliar verses of the song as well as the chorus at the Irish games in that year's World Cup finals.

The 'Soldier's Song' appears to have been written in 1907, though Kearney himself suggested it was actually penned in 1909 or later and became popular with members of the Irish Volunteers as a marching song. Kearney was a house painter by profession; his sister Kathleen would later marry another painter, Stephen Behan, making Kearney the uncle of Brendan and Dominic Behan.

Kearney joined the Gaelic League in 1901 – Sean O'Casey was one of his pupils in Irish language classes – and he took the Irish Republican Brotherhood oath in 1903. He was actively involved in the 1916 Rising and the War of Independence, becoming a personal friend of Michael Collins. Later he would take the Free State side in the Civil War, a move that certainly did no harm in the choice of his song as national anthem by the Cumann na nGaedheal government of W. T. Cosgrave. He was a witness to the death of Michael Collins in Béal na Bláth in August 1922 while travelling in the lead vehicle in the ill-fated convoy.

There is some dispute as to whether Kearney earned royalties for the writing of 'The Soldier's Song'. He did receive some money from publishers for the original composition but not from the state when the song became the national anthem. Heeney, the composer of the music, had died in straitened circumstances in 1911. When Kearney applied for royalties he was informed by the state that it was the melody and not the lyrics that constituted the anthem. Later, under threat of a royalty suit from Kearney and Heeney's brother, the state agreed to buy out the copyright in 1933 for one thousand pounds. They had to do it all over again, this time for two thousand five hundred, in 1965, after changes in copyright law.

But that was of no benefit to Kearney. He had, like his collaborator Patrick Heeney, died in relative poverty in 1944. He is buried in Glasnevin Cemetery with Thomas Ashe, who died on hunger strike in 1917, and Pearse Beasley.

Peadar Kearney, author of the, now rather unfamiliar, English language version of the Irish national anthem, 'The Soldier's Song', was born, one hundred and thirty-one years ago, on this day.

Broadcast 12 December 2014

11 December 1920
The Burning of Cork by the
Auxiliaries

The events of the night of the 11th and the morning of 12th December 1920 in Cork probably had their origins in the killing of seventeen members of the Royal Irish Constabulary on 28 November in Kilmichael. Of course these were not any ordinary members of the RIC, an organisation not greatly beloved of the plain people of Ireland in the first place.

The victims of Tom Barry's flying column at Kilmichael were members of the RIC Auxiliary force, recruited in the summer of 1920 from former and serving British army officers and touted as an elite counter-insurgency group. Counter insurgents they undoubtedly were, but their elite status took something of a drubbing as an IRA unit, wiped out a detachment of the force that became reviled in Ireland as 'the Auxies', a week after Bloody Sunday in Dublin.

What happened in Cork on 11 December, however, had a more proximate cause. The local IRA had observed that a force of Auxiliaries always left Victoria barracks on the outskirts of Cork and headed for the city centre at 8.00 p.m. every evening. An ambush was laid for them at Dillon's Cross which led to the death of one of the RIC 'Temporary Cadets', as they were formally known.

In the first wave of retaliation the Auxiliaries entered a local pub, terrorised the occupants, seized one of them, and in an egregious exhibition of military valour, stripped him naked and forced him to sing 'God Save the King' in the middle of the road. That was only the start of their nocturnal frolic.

At 9.30 p.m. they returned to Dillon's Cross, raided a number of houses, forced the occupants into the street and burned down their homes. The spree of mindless violence then continued in the city centre. There the Auxiliaries were joined by their only slightly more wholesome cousins, the Black and Tans. Together, in and out of uniform, they went on the rampage. They set Grant's department store alight; when the fire brigade arrived to fight the blaze, the firemen were prevented from doing their jobs by the Temporary Cadets and their allies – nicknamed, appropriately, after a pack of hounds. The fire fighters were threatened, shot at, and their hoses were cut.

At 4.00 a.m. Cork City Hall and the Carnegie Library went up in flames. In terms of historical records, this did for Cork what Ernie O'Malley later allegedly accomplished on a national scale when the Public Record Office in the Four Courts was atomised during the Civil War. When more fire brigade units arrived they were denied access to water by the security forces and were also fired upon when they attempted to do their jobs. At some point that night two members of the IRA, the brothers Con and Jeremiah Delany, were taken from their beds and shot out of hand.

In all, five acres of the city were destroyed, comprising forty business premises and three hundred homes. Over three million pounds worth of damage was done – which equates to around two hundred million euros today. Two thousand people were left out of work.

The British government blamed the entire episode on the IRA and were aided and abetted in this by the Roman Catholic Bishop of Cork, Daniel Cohalan, who threated to excommunicate IRA volunteers who continued their involvement in the War of Independence. His Grace was accused by Cork politicians of 'adding insult to injury'. Ironically, the only report into the affair, sanctioned by the British government, took the opposite tack and pointed the finger at K Company of the Auxiliaries, based at Victoria barracks. When the British government refused to publish the so-called 'Strickland' report the Prime Minister and Irish Secretary were berated in the House of Commons by one of the few remaining Irish Party MPs, T. P. O'Connor, who sat for one of the Liverpool constituencies.

K Company of the Auxiliaries thereafter sported burnt corks in their hats as a provocative reminder of their penchant for pyromania and wreaking havoc. The unit was, to the regret of none, other than its members, disbanded in March 1921, four months before the truce of the War of Independence.

Much of the centre of the city of Cork was razed to the ground by the British security forces, ninety-five years ago, on this day.

Broadcast 11 December 2015

5 December 1921
British Delegation Issues
Ultimatum in the Anglo-Irish Treaty
Negotiations

In July 1921, after more than two years of sporadic, vicious and often ferocious violence, the British government, under external and internal pressure, conceded that Sinn Féin, Dáil Éireann and its military wing, the Irish Republican Army, were not going to go away. They sought and secured a truce during which agreement might be reached on the future governance of the twenty-six counties of Ireland where the Anglo-Irish war had been raging.

That process began, inauspiciously, from a republican point of view, on 12 July 1921 when Eamon de Valera led a delegation to London for preliminary talks. In fact most of the talking took place in a series of bilateral meetings between de Valera and British Prime Minister Lloyd George. These encounters with the famous 'Welsh Wizard' may have been what prompted the Irish leader to absent himself from the full-blown talks that finally began in October. During their *tête-à-têtes,* Lloyd George had made it clear that the Irish *sine qua non* of a republic was not going to form part of any negotiations.

Whatever the most compelling reason was for his decision not to travel, it was Michael Collins, increasingly being seen as a serious leadership rival to de Valera, who was given the task of heading the delegation, with Arthur Griffith as his principal associate. The delegates were given plenipotentiary powers to 'negotiate and conclude ... a treaty or treaties of settlement, association and accommodation between Ireland and the community of nations known as the British Commonwealth'. However, Collins was also handed a note from de Valera instructing him that reference had to be made to the Cabinet in Dublin before any agreement was signed.

Leading the formidable British delegation was David Lloyd George himself, aided by, among others, future Prime Minister Winston Churchill. Offering valuable administrative and advisory support was the Prime Minister's secretary Thomas Jones. Both Lloyd George and Jones were Welsh speakers and were not averse to rattling the Irish delegation by breaking into their native language with each other in the course of negotiations.

Lloyd George concentrated on developing a personal relationship with Collins and Griffith. The refusal of the British to concede a republic had led de Valera to devise an ingenious form of external association that recognised the Crown while mimicking many of the attributes of an independent republic. This approach, more or less, passed muster with the British.

The issue of Ulster was more problematic. The Irish had been told to break off discussions on the issue of partition – which is somewhat ironic as it played a negligible part in the later Treaty debates in Dáil Éireann. However, Lloyd George managed to persuade Griffith in a private meeting *not* to break on Ulster. He was later held to this guarantee at a crucial point in the talks.

Collins was also having problems with his fellow plenipotentiaries. The secretary, Erskine Childers, objected to any major concession on a republic, while two of the delegates, Robert Barton, first cousin of Childers, and the London-based solicitor George Gavan Duffy, were getting restless at their exclusion from the many private meetings involving Collins and Griffith.

As the talks moved from November into December 1921, a combination of threats and cajolery began to wear down the Irish plenipotentiaries. Eventually, on the evening of 5 December, they were told by Lloyd George to take or leave what was on offer from Britain or risk bearing personal responsibility for the resumption of, in the British Prime Minister's own words, 'immediate and terrible war'. The Irish delegation succumbed and signed the Treaty the following day. Later Collins wrote prophetically to a friend 'early this morning I signed my death warrant. I thought at the time how odd, how ridiculous – a bullet may just as well have done the job five years ago'.

The British delegation to the Anglo-Irish talks threatened to resume the Anglo-Irish war, ninety-three years ago, on this day.

Broadcast 5 December 2014

19 December 1973
Mary McGee Wins Supreme Court
Case Allowing Her to Import
Contraceptives

The fallout from a Supreme Court decision made in December 1973 led to two of the greatest and most surreal clichés in Irish political and legal history, as well as the belated introduction of the concept of modernity into Irish life. The clichés are the immortal 'an Irish solution to an Irish problem' and 'bona fide family planning purposes'.

I'm referring of course to the celebrated and game-changing decision in the *McGee v Attorney General and the Revenue Commissioners* case which, in effect, legalised contraception in Ireland while leaving it up to our courageous legislators to work out the details.

The McGee in question was the previously unheralded Mary McGee who, it emerged in court proceedings, was 'a young married woman who is living, with a slender income, in the cramped quarters of a mobile home with her husband and four infant children, and ... is faced with a considerable risk of death or crippling paralysis if she becomes pregnant'.

Mary McGee had suffered a stroke and temporary paralysis during one of her pregnancies and had been advised by her doctor to avoid any future pregnancy and to use a diaphragm and spermicidal jelly as contraception. In 1970s Ireland she had to secure supplies of the jelly abroad and import them via the postal service. When one batch was confiscated by customs officials she sued the state, claiming that such seizures placed her life in jeopardy. She was forced, by a series of unfavourable judicial decisions, to take her case all the way to the Supreme Court.

There, by a majority of four to one, the court ruled that the Revenue Commissioners via the Irish Customs service had interfered with her constitutional rights to marital privacy. One of the country's greatest jurists, Justice Brian Walsh, in his judgement, observed that:

> *Both Aristotle and the Christian philosophers have regarded justice as the highest human virtue. The virtue of prudence was also esteemed by Aristotle as by the philosophers of the Christian world. But the great additional virtue introduced by Christianity was that of charity, not the charity which consists of giving to the deserving, for that is justice, but the charity which is also called mercy.*

The decision, contrary to popular belief, did not legalise contraception in Ireland, but it did put an onus on legislators to take action. This they did with startling tardiness. The Fine Gael-Labour coalition, elected in 1973, attempted legislation in 1974 but it was voted down by, among others, the Taoiseach of the day, Liam Cosgrave. He opposed his own government's measure but didn't bother to tell anyone of his plans until he trooped into the 'Níl' lobby with the entire Fianna Fáil party and Fine Gael Education Minister Richard Burke.

It was left to the then Minister for Health Charles J. Haughey in 1979 to introduce a highly restrictive bill or, if you prefer, a poisoned chalice, which he famously described as 'an Irish solution to an Irish problem' (Immortal cliché number one). Contraceptives were to be available on prescription only and access was restricted to those who could establish that they were being used for (Great cliché number two) 'bona fide family planning purposes' – i.e. you had to be married. That restriction was amended in 1983 but it wasn't until the spread of AIDS in the 1990s that access became general.

The unassuming, unheralded and heroic Mary McGee won her case against the Revenue Commissioners, forty-one years ago, on this day.

Broadcast 19 December 2014